Edgar Cayce on

Angels and the Angelic Forces

Selected Books by Kevin J. Todeschi

Edgar Cayce on Angels and the Angelic Forces
Kevin J. Todeschi, MA

Non-Fiction

The Best Dream Book Ever
Contemporary Cayce (co-author)
Divine Encounters
Dreams, Images and Symbols
Edgar Cayce's ESP
Edgar Cayce on the Akashic Records
Edgar Cayce on Auras & Colors (co-author)
Edgar Cayce on Mastering Your Spiritual Growth
Edgar Cayce on Reincarnation and Family Karma
Edgar Cayce on Soul Mates
Edgar Cayce on Soul Symbolism
Edgar Cayce on Vibrations
Edgar Cayce's Twelve Lessons in Personal Spirituality

Fiction

A Persian Tale
The Reincarnation of Clara
The Rest of the Noah Story

Edgar Cayce on

Angels and the Angelic Forces

Kevin J. Todeschi, MA

A.R.E. Press • Virginia Beach • Virginia

A.R.E. Press
215 67th Street
Virginia Beach, VA 23451-2061

ISBN-13: 978-0-87604-973-0

All biblical quotes come from the King James Version of the Bible.

Cover design by Christine Fulcher

Be not forgetful to entertain strangers: for thereby some have entertained angels unawares.   Hebrews 13:2

Contents

Preface
A Brief History of Angels

Just what are guardian angels, archangels, and divine messengers? Even the words can produce comfort, reassurance, and hope, for they suggest the presence of celestial beings who have concern for humankind and are somehow involved with the lives and activities of all individuals. Are these emissaries of light spiritual beings that come directly from God? Are they somehow responsible for bringing information, guidance, and even a healing presence into people's lives? Were angels only a part of the spiritual history of the past, or do they continue to maintain an interaction with humans even now? Are there both "good angels" and "fallen angels"? What role do they play in the earth? Just who and what are these divine creatures?

The word "angel" comes from the Greek word "angelos," which means messenger. According to the Greek philosopher Plato (ca. 427–347 BC), from birth each human soul has the capacity to be guided by a portion of its divine or higher self. This divine influence might also be perceived as individualized lesser gods, messengers, and "daemons." These lesser gods and daemons are the intermediaries between Zeus and the world of mortals. They are charged with helping the human creature return to its divine origins. When an individual soul follows the positive aspects of these divine influences, that soul is nourished and grows closer to the heavenly realms; when it does not, it may too easily fall sway to ugliness and evil, experiencing digression in the process. In the words of Plato's *Phaedrus*, the process is described, as follows:

> Now by these excellences especially is the soul's plumage nour-
> ished and fostered, while by their opposites, even by ugliness
> and evil, it is wasted and destroyed. And behold, there in the
> heaven Zeus, mighty leader, drives his winged team. First of the
> host of gods and daemons he proceeds, ordering all things and
> caring therefor, and the host follows after him ...
>
> Phaedrus 246e-247a[1]

Jewish mysticism suggests that aspects of angel lore can be traced back to both the Babylonians and the Persians.[2] In fact, the Persian faith of Zoroastrianism details the existence of both archangels and a personal guardian angel, called a Fravashi, which is essentially the personal spirit guide for every single soul. Another similarity is that the Persian destructive spirit, Ahriman, possesses similarities to the fallen angel, Lucifer. Depending upon one's interpretation, the first mention of an angel in Judeo–Christian scriptures may be related to a fallen angel taking the form of a serpent and tempting Eve to eat the fruit of a forbidden tree, resulting in Adam and Eve being evicted from the Garden of Eden:

> Now the serpent was more subtil than any beast of the
> field which the Lord God had made. And he said unto the
> woman, Yea, hath God said, Ye shall not eat of every tree
> of the garden?
> And the woman said unto the serpent, We may eat of the

---

[1] Edith Hamilton and Huntington Cairns, ed., *Plato: The Collected Dialogues* (New York: Pantheon Books, 1961).

[2] *The Jewish Encyclopedia: A Descriptive Record of the History, Religion, Literature and Customs of the Jewish People from Earliest Times to the Present Day* (London: Funk and Wagnalls Co., 1901), 589.

fruit of the trees of the garden:

But of the fruit of the tree which *is* in the midst of the garden, God hath said, Ye shall not eat of it, neither shall ye touch it, lest ye die.

And the serpent said unto the woman, Ye shall not surely die: Gen. 3:1-4

Later within the same chapter, we find the first mention of benevolent angels in the form of Cherubim (the most frequently mentioned type of angel), who are asked to stand guard to prevent Adam and Eve from returning to the Garden:

Therefore the Lord God sent him forth from the garden of Eden, to till the ground from whence he was taken.

So he drove out the man; and he placed at the east of the garden of Eden Cherubims, and a flaming sword which turned every way, to keep the way of the tree of life.

Gen. 3:23-24

According to the interpretation of some, fallen angels actually make their second appearance after the Flood when they become physically tempted by the beauty of some of Noah's descendants, as is illustrated by: "the sons of God saw the daughters of men that they *were* fair; and they took them wives of all which they chose." (Gen. 6:2)

Setting aside these earliest references in Genesis, the first mention of an angelic messenger in scripture occurs in Genesis 16. According to the tale, Abram and Sarai were aged and had never been able to conceive children. Feeling sorry for her husband's lack of progeny, Sarai gave him her younger Egyptian handmaid, Hagar, with whom to conceive. Unfortunately for Hagar, when the younger woman became pregnant, Sarai became angry and treated her harshly, causing Hagar to flee the household. It was while she was resting at a desert spring that "an angel of the Lord" appeared to her, encouraged her to return home, and correctly prophesied that she would conceive a son and name him Ishmael.

Soon after Sarai and Abram had been renamed by God as Sarah and Abraham, three angels disguised as mortal men made an appearance and correctly predicted that the elderly couple would soon have a son of their own and name him Isaac. (Gen. 18) In fact, Abraham was told by an angelic messenger that God had ordained his descendants to become as numerous "as the stars of the heaven, and as the sand which is upon the sea shore." (Gen. 22:17) The prophecy became realized in that the religions of Judaism, Islam, and Christianity all trace their roots to Abraham—perhaps explaining, in part, the similarities in "angelology" among these three faiths.

The final mention of an angelic encounter in the Bible occurs in the closing chapters of Revelation (chapters 21–22) during the Apostle John's visionary experience on Patmos when an angelic messenger shows him a depiction of the "new Jerusalem" as it descends from the clouds. Between the first mention and the last, scripture discusses angels nearly 300 times but surprisingly only two archangels are ever named: Michael and Gabriel.

History records numerous angelic experiences across religious boundaries. Both Michael and Gabriel are also mentioned in the Quran. In fact, a belief in angels is one of Islam's six articles of faith. In addition to a variety of angels, including guardian angels, the Quran names two additional archangels that also have an importance in both Jewish and Christian traditions: Raphael and Azrael. Perhaps most importantly for Islam, it was an encounter between Mohammed and the angel Gabriel that led to the writing of the Quran in the sixth century.

According to legend, during his merchant travels Mohammed became distressed that God's revelations through various prophets like Abraham, Moses, and Jesus had become corrupted with the passage of time. Deeply troubled, Mohammed sought solace in a desert cave and spent months in prayer, fasting, and meditation. During that period, Mohammed was awakened by the voice of the angel Gabriel who presented a cloth covered with writing for Mohammed to read. Despite Mohammed's confession that he was illiterate and unable to read, divine intervention made it possible, and the prophet "instantly felt his understanding illumined with celestial light, and read what was written on the cloth, which contained the decrees of God, as afterwards promulgated in the Koran."[3]

Approximately 100 years after the archangel Gabriel's first appear-

---

[3]Washington Irving, *Life of Mahomet* (New York: E.P Dutton and Company, Inc. 1915), 37.

ance to Mohammed, another archangel would make several attempts to communicate information from the realm of spirit to the mortal world of humankind. According to legend, in the year 708 the archangel Michael appeared in a dream to Aubert, bishop of Avranches, France. The archangel instructed the bishop to build a chapel on top of Mont Tombe, one mile off the coast of Normandy. The absurdity of the request caused the bishop to ignore the angel's command. It occurred a second time and still the bishop did nothing. Finally, the archangel Michael appeared in person and struck the bishop with a blazing angelic finger, reportedly leaving a permanent indentation in Aubert's skull. The bishop needed no further encouragement to begin his task, and finally the chapel that would become Mont Saint Michel five hundred years later was begun.

Catholic Church history details the experiences of numerous saints whose angelic experiences assisted them with their missions; perhaps one of the most well-known is the story of Joan of Arc (1412–1431). Born into a peasant family, she rose to prominence as a leader of the French resistance against the English occupation of her homeland during the Hundred Years' War. Joan claimed that she had first heard the voice of the archangel Michael when she was only thirteen. The archangel became a frequent presence in her life. Although female and lacking any military training, Michael told her that she had been chosen to help liberate France against the English. By the age of eighteen, she was leader of the French army and proved victorious over the English at Orleans. Her efforts enabled Charles VII to become King of France. Later, she was captured by the English, and because she refused to deny her claims of speaking to both the archangel and other saints, she was burned at the stake for witchcraft when she was only nineteen years old.[4]

Swedish mystic, author, theologian, and scientist Emanuel Swedenborg (1688–1772) claimed to have innumerable personal encounters with angels. According to Swedenborg, he had countless opportunities to both see and speak with these divine beings who were very human in appearance:

---

[4]Sean Kelly and Rosemary Rogers, *Saints Preserve Us!* (New York: Random House, 1993), 152–53.

That angels are human forms, or men has been seen by me a thousand times. I have talked with them as man with man, sometimes with one, sometimes with many together; and I have seen nothing whatever in their form different from the human form …

From all my experience, which is now of many years, I am able to say and affirm that angels are wholly men in form, having faces, eyes, ears, bodies, arms, hands, and feet; that they see and hear one another, and in a word lack nothing whatever that belongs to men except that they are not clothed in material bodies. I have seen them in their own light, which exceeds by many degrees the noonday light of the world, and in that light all their features could be seen more distinctly and clearly than the faces of men are seen on the earth.[5]

In the United States another angelic encounter would lay the groundwork for the establishment of a religious movement in the nineteenth century by Joseph Smith (1805–1844) of upstate New York. Smith detailed how a series of visions beginning in 1823 encouraged him to restore true Christianity to God's kingdom on earth. In time, an angel named Moroni would reveal a set of golden plates that were written in an undecipherable form of hieroglyphics. The angel also provided Smith with a set of "seer stones"—the Biblical equivalent of the Urim and Thummim—that were to be used for translating the plates. Joseph Smith translated the ancient plates shown to him by Moroni, eventually resulting in the publication of the *Book of Mormon* in 1830. Mormons believe that rather than being a separate form of creation, angels are essentially the spirits of human beings who have been resurrected or have yet to be born. For example, one doctrine of Mormon faith is that Adam in death and resurrection became the archangel Michael.[6]

Christian mystic, priest, and Catholic Saint Padre Pio (1887–1968) was known for his miraculous healings, his possession of the stigmata (the

[5]Emanuel Swedenborg, *Heaven and Its Wonders and Hell* (New York: Swedenborg Foundation, 1964), 38–9.

[6]*Doctrine and Covenants* (Salt Lake City: Church of Jesus Christ of Latter Day Saints, 2013), Covenant 27:11.

wounds of Christ), and his ability to communicate with angels. He often attested to the reality of each individual possessing a guardian angel charged with assisting and caring for that person. In 1919, in order to test the validity of Padre Pio's visionary claims, one of his superiors wrote a letter to him in Greek—a language totally unknown to the young priest. When Pio was able to understand what had been written, his superior asked how that was possible, and the younger priest stated, "My guardian angel explained it all to me."[7]

Later in life he became known for his loving kindness and his ability to bring comfort to thousands. Individuals who sincerely asked for his help or guidance became his "spiritual children." Pio often encouraged them to simply "send me your guardian angel" whenever they needed help or spiritual assistance. One of these spiritual children was English gentleman, speaker, and author, Cecil Humphrey–Smith, who often had the opportunity to visit Padre Pio in his hometown of San Giovanni Rotondo in southern Italy.

According to reports, one day Smith was seriously injured in a car accident far away from his friend the priest. Concerned about the injuries, another friend of Smith's went to the post office to send a telegram to Padre Pio asking for prayers. To the friend's surprise when he reached the post office, there was a telegram from Padre Pio to Cecil Humphrey–Smith assuring him that he would be prayed for. Months later, when Smith had recovered and found occasion to visit Padre Pio in person, he asked how the priest had known about the accident, to which Padre Pio replied: "Do you think the angels go as slowly as the planes?"[8]

Another Christian mystic and clairvoyant who communicated with the angelic realms, as well as sprites and fairies, was Flower Newhouse (born Mildred Sechler; 1909–1994). Through lectures, publications, educational programs, and the founding of Questhaven Retreat Center in San Diego, California, Flower dedicated her life to sharing with others all she had come to know of the angelic realms.

By her own account, her first encounter with these spiritual beings

[7]Fr. Alesslio Parente, O.F.M., Cap, *"Send Me Your Guardian Angel" Padre Pio* (Amsterdam, NY: The Noteworthy Co, 1983), 32.

[8]Ibid., 81.

occurred when she was only six years old and stood against the railing of the Staten Island Ferry on its way to the New York Harbor. Suddenly, her face became illuminated with enthusiasm and joy, and she pointed over the railing and exclaimed, "Oh, look at the beautiful fairies!"[9] Through her young eyes she could see dozens of tiny fairies, called "water sprites," dancing atop the water's surface. With a friend at the time, she was shocked when she realized that her friend could not see the same thing. The fact that her visionary experiences seemed to be hers alone would eventually lead her to the unmistakable conclusion that she "saw a world that other people didn't."[10]

Raised in a Christian background with a strong Quaker influence, Mildred had long believed in the presence of guardian angels. Therefore, it came as no surprise to her when, at the age of ten, her guardian angel appeared to her and stated, "It is now my task to take the responsibility of your life's instruction."[11] At the age of thirteen, following the prompting of her guardian, Mildred explained to her mother and sister (her father had died years before) that she no longer wished to be called "Mildred" but instead "Flower"—the name would stick for the rest of her life.

As she grew, so did her clairvoyant abilities. She could see the human aura as easily as she could see the energy associated with thought and feeling. The world she witnessed became one of boundless light, pulsating with the spark of Creation. In time, the entire angelic hierarchy became as visible to her as the mundane world was to others. The life forms Flower perceived included all imaginable creatures from "elementals" and "nature beings" to "devas" and "Archangels." She would come to realize that in addition to guardian angels for individuals, there were angelic beings for every plant, every creature, every aspect of nature, and even every country. On one occasion, while discussing the angels she could see caring for humanity, Flower had the following to say:

---

[9]Stephen Isaac, *Songs from the House of Pilgrimage* (Boston: Branden Press, 1971), 45.

[10]Ibid., 46.

[11]Ibid., 50.

All Angels are beautiful beyond imagining. Masculine Angels are overpowering in their magnificent power, joyousness and love. Feminine Angels change anyone who sees them through their transforming embodiments of truth, devotion, and grace. Guardian Angels are no exception; they are all the beauties of love ... Their hair and eye colors resemble human colors ...

Guardians are with their wards during every day of their earth lives. They may grow frustrated over their charges' perversities, but they never tire. Seventy or eighty years are like days to them, for there is no time in the mental plane where their consciousness usually resides ... One has the same Guardian throughout every incarnation ...

Watcher Angels, on the other hand, are not with their charges constantly. These Angels are in training to be Guardians, and they have several probationary humans in their care. Watchers closely supervise their charges when meeting a testing of evil forces. They stay to help their wards through these times by prompting, uplifting, inspiring, and teaching. Constantly aware of each charge's thoughts and circumstances, Watcher Angels are able to accompany each person in their care during times of need.[12]

Throughout her life, Flower Newhouse believed that all of Creation acted at its best as it served and worshipped God. Not only was this worship of the Divine the ultimate purpose for every individual, regardless of his or her religious background, but it was also the natural calling for every kingdom of Creation, including angels, devas, elementals, and fairies.

The most documented psychic of all time, Edgar Cayce (1877–1945), was once asked about Flower Newhouse and her ability to discuss information about the angelic realms. In one reading, Cayce described her as "a most excellent channel."[13] In addition to being contemporaries

---

[12]Flower Newhouse, *Here Are Your Answers (Volume III)* (Escondido, CA: Christward Ministry, 1983), 131–32.

[13]Edgar Cayce reading 1152-11, August 3, 1941. Note: the Edgar Cayce readings have been numbered to maintain confidentiality. The first set of numbers (e.g., "1152") refers to the individual or group for whom the reading was given. The second set of numbers (e.g., "11") refers to the number in the series from which the reading is taken. For example, 1152-11 identifies the reading as the eleventh one given to the individual assigned number 1152.

during the early portion of the twentieth century and the fact that both demonstrated clairvoyant abilities, Cayce's own life entailed personal experiences with the angelic realms and a thorough discussion of these spiritual beings in literally hundreds of psychic readings given to other people. A Christian mystic and founder of the Association for Research and Enlightenment, Inc. (www.EdgarCayce.org), for forty-three years of his adult life, Edgar Cayce possessed the ability to lie on a couch, close his eyes, fold his hands over his stomach, and put himself into an altered state of consciousness in which virtually any information was available to him. Cayce's uncanny accuracy is evidenced by literally hundreds of books that discuss his amazing work, an exploration of literally thousands of topics, and an astonishing readings' database consisting of twenty-four million words!

In terms of angelic encounters, an early experience in 1890 would forever shape Cayce's life direction. As a boy he had vowed to read the Bible once through for every year of his life. Called a "peculiar child" by neighbors and other children, he often found solace in the woods reading the Bible. It was here he could find peace from his childhood concerns, including the fact that he was not a good student—a problem made worse by the fact that his stern father was often his tutor.

One day Cayce had just finished rereading the biblical story of Manoah, in which an "angel of God" appeared and foretold Manoah that he and his wife would have a son and name him Samson. (Judges 13) After reading the story, young Edgar hurried home and had a challenging experience with his own father over his inability to memorize a spelling lesson. Unable to remember even some of the simplest words, Cayce recalled that when it was time for bed, he prayed for direction so that his life would have a purpose:

> Kneeling by my bed that night, I prayed again that God would show me that He loved me, that He would give me the ability to do something for my fellow man which would show to them His love …
>
> I was not yet asleep when the vision first began, but I felt as if I were being lifted up. A glorious light as of the rising morning sun seemed to fill the whole room, and a figure appeared at the foot of my bed. I was sure it was my mother, and I called to her

but she didn't answer. For the moment I was frightened, climbed out of bed and went to my mother's room. No she hadn't called. Almost immediately after I returned to my couch, the figure came again. Then it seemed all gloriously bright—an angel, or what, I knew not; but gently, patiently, it said: "Thy prayers are heard. You will have your wish. Remain faithful. Be true to yourself. Help the sick, the afflicted." [14]

The next day, after enduring several hours of his father's tutoring and being repeatedly rebuffed for his stupidity and inability to memorize a spelling lesson, an exhausted Edgar asked to be able to rest for five minutes. His father left the room in disgust and Cayce laid his head on his speller to go to sleep, just as he heard the angelic woman's voice comfort him with: "Rely on the promise." When Cayce woke up, not only did he know the lesson but he could spell every word in the book: "Not only was I able to spell all the words in the lesson, but any word in that particular book; not only spell them, but tell on what page and what line each word could be found and how it was marked."

Years later, when Edgar Cayce was an adult, a woman who had received numerous readings from him wrote to ask for details on his experiences as a child when he had "playmates that no one could see but yourself." Part of Cayce's written response was as follows:

> ...I have never attempted to put those experiences in writing. So, if my letter appears somewhat disconnected or unreasonable, know that it is because of a physically developed body (and possibly a sane mind) attempting to keep within the bounds of reason. Except the fairy stories of Grimm and Hans Andersen, I have never read of others' experiences ...As to just what was the first experience, I don't know. The one that appears at present to be among the first, was when I was possibly eighteen or twenty months old. I had a playhouse in the back of an old garden, among the honeysuckle and other flowers. At that particular time much of this garden had grown up in tall reeds,

14 A. Robert Smith, compiler and editor. *The Lost Memoirs of Edgar Cayce* (Virginia Beach, VA: A.R.E. Press, 1997), 14–15.

as I remember. I had made a little shelter of the tops of the reeds, and had been assisted by an unseen playmate in weaving or fastening them together so they would form a shelter. On pretty days I played there. One afternoon my mother came down the garden walk calling me. My playmate (who appeared to me to be about the same size as myself) was with me. It had never occurred to me that he was not real, or that he wasn't one of the neighbors' children, until my mother spoke and asked me my playmate's name. I turned to ask him but he disappeared. For a time this disturbed my mother somewhat, and she questioned me at length. I remember crying because she had spied upon me several times, and each time the playmate would disappear. About a year or eighteen months later, this was changed considerably—as to the number of playmates. We had moved to another country home. Here I had two favorite places where I played with these unseen people. One (very peculiarly) was in an old graveyard where the cedar trees had grown up. Under a cedar tree, whose limbs had grown very close to the ground, I made another little retreat, where—with these playmates—I gathered bits of colored glass, beautifully colored leaves and things of that nature from time to time. But, what disturbed me was that I didn't know where they came from nor why they left when some of my family approached. The other retreat was a favorite old strawstack that I used to slide down. This was on the opposite side of the road (main highway) from where we lived, and in front of the house. The most outstanding experience (and one that I am sure disturbed her much) was when my mother looked out a window and saw children sliding down this strawstack with me. Of course, I had a lovely little retreat dug out under the side of the straw ring, in which we often sat and discussed the mighty problems of a three or four-year-old child. As my mother looked out, she called to ask who were the children playing with me. I realized I didn't know their names. How were they dressed, you ask? There were boys and girls. It would be impossible (at this date) to describe their dress, figure or face, yet it didn't then—nor does it now—occur to me that they were any different from myself, except that they had the ability to appear or disappear as our moods changed. Just once I looked out the window from the house and saw the fairies there, beckoning me to come and play. That time also my mother saw them very plainly, but she didn't make any objection to my going out to play with them. This experience, as I remember now, lasted during a whole season—or summer. A few years afterwards (when I had grown to be six or seven years old) our home was in a little wood. Here I learned to talk with the trees, or it appeared that they talked with me. I even yet hold that anyone may hear voices, apparently coming from a tree, if willing to choose a tree (a living tree, not a dead one) and sit against it for fifteen to twenty minutes each day (the same time each day) for twenty days. This was my experience. I chose a very lovely tree, and around it I played with my playmates that came (who then seemed very much smaller than I). We built a beautiful bower of hazelnut branches, redwood, dogwood and the like, with wild violets, Jack-in-the-Pulpit, and many of the wild mosses that seemed to be especially drawn to this partic-ular little place where I met my friends to talk with—the little elves of the trees. How often this came, I don't know. We lived there for several years. It was there that I read the Bible through the first time, that I learned to pray, that I had many visions or experiences; not only of visioning the elves but what seemed to me to be the hosts that must have appeared to the people of old, as recorded in Genesis particularly. In this little bower there was never any intrusion from those outside. It was here that I read the first letter from a girlfriend. It was here that I went to pray when my grandmother died, whom I loved so dearly and who had meant so much to me. To describe these elves of the trees, the fairies of the woods, or—to me—the angels or hosts, with all their beautiful and glorious surroundings, would be almost a sacrilege. They have meant, and do yet, so very much to me that they are as rather the sacred experiences that we do not speak of—any more than we would of our first kiss, and the like. Why do I draw such comparisons? There are, no doubt, physical manifestations that are a counterpart or an expression of all the unseen forces about us, yet we have closed our eyes and our ears to the songs of the spheres, so that we are unable again to hear the voices or to see the forms take shape and minister—yea strengthen us—day by day!   Report 464-12

In 1928, while giving a reading on the work of Cayce's organization, an angelic encounter occurred when a booming voice suddenly spoke through the sleeping Cayce with the announcement: "I AM MICHAEL, LORD OF THE WAY." It would be the first of more than a dozen occasions when the archangel Michael would use Edgar Cayce as a channel for information he wished to share with spiritual seekers.

On another occasion in June 1936, Edgar Cayce was out in garden when suddenly he heard a "buzzing noise" in the air. He looked to see a chariot in the sky with four white horses and a rider and suddenly an armored angelic figure appeared behind him. Cayce described the individual as follows: "His countenance was like the light, armor as silver or aluminum. He raised his hand in salute and said, 'The chariot of the Lord and the horsemen thereof.'" (Report 1196-2) Cayce's secretary would note in the file: "I heard Edgar Cayce say that he dropped his hoe and when he reached up his hand to mop his brow his hand came down all red looking, as if he were sweating blood." Hugh Lynn Cayce [Edgar's eldest son] said that his father ran against him in the front hall, white and shaking, on the way to his chair in the living room. The angelic vision seemed to foretell the United States entry into a World War five–and–a–half years later.

In addition to these personal experiences, throughout the decades that Edgar Cayce gave readings on spiritual growth and personal development, angels were discussed on literally hundreds of occasions. Questions like: "How do angels help humanity?" "Does everyone have a guardian angel?" "What is the symbolic meaning of angels in the Book of Revelation?" and repeated references to the meaning of Psalm 91:11: "For he shall give his angels charge over thee . . . " were explored frequently. As the readings often examined epochs in history, there were also instances when the biblical tales of angels came alive with additional insights that had not been recorded previously.

This book was written in an effort to explore the subject of angels and angelic encounters in the lives of individuals. In addition to detailing the insights and information that came through Edgar Cayce, the most documented psychic of all time, it examines contemporary stories of angelic encounters in the lives of everyday people. What can these experiences tell us about the nature of God and the workings of spirit? What can we learn from angels and the angelic forces? Is there a role for angelic messengers even in our lives today? Perhaps the ultimate lesson is that although we are spiritual beings having a physical experience, the spiritual realm is never very far from us. We are very much a part of spirit, even when we are in the earth.

Kevin J. Todeschi

1

Edgar Cayce on Angels

"Are angels real?" "Does everyone have an angel?" "If angels are actual beings, what role do they play in the lives of individuals?" Answers to these questions and many others can be explored in hundreds of Edgar Cayce readings given to individuals over several decades. Many of these insights can be found in readings that deal with personal spiritual growth. Much like the Parable of the Prodigal Son (Luke 15:11–32), the Cayce material suggests that each individual's life unfoldment will eventually lead to an awareness that the ultimate journey is a journey Home—one in which we become aware of our true spiritual nature and our connection to the One Creator we all have in common. The Cayce readings confirm that there are personal guardian angels charged with the responsibility of overseeing this journey for each and every soul.

In addition to guardian angels, there are angelic beings who seem to be part of a collective work—overseeing a task or a responsibility that may come into play for individuals depending upon their individual choices and actions. These angelic beings seem to oversee patterns of behavior to which the human creature has an affinity. Three of the most common patterns that the soul seems susceptible to on its journey through space and time are: choosing to live in alignment with Divine will, choosing selfishness and personal rebelliousness and therefore remaining ignorant of the soul's divine nature, and choosing to follow the patterns of karmic memory rather than growing in awareness through spiritual grace. Through their own free will, individuals ultimately choose their path of life unfoldment, and regardless of that choice, the angelic realms are there to help oversee each individual's direction.

From Cayce's perspective, there are also a variety of "spirit guides" who can have an influence upon individuals, again based upon choices that the soul is making in life. Many examples of the role of guides is explored by the Cayce information; however, two things quickly become apparent in the readings dealing with spirit guides. The first is that each individual attracts to himself or herself guides that have an affinity to that soul's current level of development. In other words, as an individual grows along the spiritual path, the level of guide and guidance available to that individual grows as well. Cayce repeatedly told individuals that just because someone was a spirit guide did not mean that the guide was any more knowledgeable than the person that guide was trying to help. The second premise in the Cayce material dealing with guides is that individuals should not attempt to contact these spirit guides firsthand. Instead, the readings encouraged individuals to continually seek their relationship to the Creator and guides would be sent when their influence could be of help.

Taken together, the readings repeatedly confirm that angels are real and very much involved with the activities of humankind. Each individual apparently has a host of angels and spirit guides that stand ready to be of personal assistance in life. The principal role of these angelic influences is as a source of guidance and inspiration for soul growth and personal development. The long-term goal is that the Creator wants each and every soul to reawaken to its divine origins and have an awareness of its true Home.

One of the most oft-repeated quotes regarding angels that is cited in the Cayce readings is, "He has given his angels charge concerning thee, lest at any time thou dash thy foot against a stone." Originating in scripture (Psalm 91:11–12, Matt. 4:6, and Luke 4: 10–11), the readings contend that this phrase deals with the fact that the angelic realms have been charged with assisting all individuals in their passage through time and space. Whether the path is challenging or joyful, the angelic guardian is present. What is most interesting, however, is that the choices each individual makes either opens that person up to more divine guidance and angelic assistance or cuts self off from these spiritual resources. Apparently, an individual is assisted from the angelic realms more readily as that person keeps self in alignment with spiritual laws and doing the best that he or she knows to do.

For example, Cayce told a forty–five–year–old woman that she had a depth of tolerance and acceptance of other people to such an extent that she could exemplify being a friend "even to the friendless." She was encouraged to work on self-development. For as she worked on herself, she would become even more capable of assisting others, and she would also become an even greater channel of blessings to others. In reading 443–1, the advice came, "Hence, keep thine self in the way; for His ways are not past finding out. For, He has given His angels charge concerning thee, that thou dash not thy foot against a stone," suggesting that by living in accord with spiritual principles, the angels themselves would assist her in her life's direction. When she asked if she should seek outside assistance or guidance, the reading suggested that as long as she held true to her personal growth, what she needed would be provided from the Creator by way of the angelic forces. Cayce went on to say:

> . . . begin where thou art; using that thou hast in hand. And, as the applications of self in such relations bear fruit, so may the activities be expanded in the lives and experiences of those whom the entity contacts in any and all walks of life; aiding in disseminating, then, that *thou* hast found in *thine* experience to be an aid to making of self a channel of blessing to some one. For, as each soul gives out does it grow more and more and become manifested even in material things. *This* the entity may do well . . . many of those things necessary have been completed in earth's experiences in the entity's soul development. Has it not been given that the entity has learned tolerance and love?

> And it has been well said, "Though I speak with the tongues of men and of angels, and have not love, I am nothing." Love, then, is the greater blessing. *Truly* may it be said in the experience of any soul in the earth. The entity, then, is both tolerant and *lovely* in the expression of self. Seek, then through self, that the angels that have been given charge concerning thine activities may guard, guide and keep thee well.   443-1

On another occasion while giving a reading on the topics of personal development and the sixth sense (intuition), Cayce stated unequivocally that the farther an individual wandered from the spiritual path, the harder it was for that person to access intuitive guidance from the spirit realm. It was only when the individual sought instead to do the best of his or her ability that the "barriers" were somehow removed, making guidance available once again. That guidance came in a variety of ways, including hunches and advice in the sleep state. The reading went on to suggest that even when an individual strayed from the path and disregarded the things of the spirit, that individual's angelic guides remained present, standing ever ready as perhaps a mediator of assistance between the Creator and the person needing help. Cayce confirmed that the angelic guide as well as the spiritual consciousness of the self stand ever in the presence of the Divine, even when the individual had no interest in things of a spiritual nature:

> It is there! It's as to whether they desire or not! It doesn't leave but is the active force ... for has it not been said, "He has given his angels charge concerning thee, lest at any time thou dashest thy foot against a stone?" Have you heeded? Then He is near. Have you disregarded?   5754-3

Not only do angels stand ready to help any individual who sincerely seeks to become his or her best Self, but the angelic realms also seem to be readily available to assist groups and organizations that hold as their purpose somehow being of spiritual assistance to humankind. During one of the "Work readings" that explore ways to carry on the work of Edgar Cayce and the association he founded, a reading confirmed that the A.R.E. organization could be helped by angels as long as it held to its spiritual ideals.

> But as has been given as respecting individuals, "He hath given His angels charge concerning thee, lest at any time ye dash your foot against a stone." It's just as applicable in any group organization as it is in an individual entity. Yet there becomes in the practical application more of a confusion unless the *ideals* and the purposes that are of a spiritual nature are held to.   254-92

During the same reading, Cayce went on to say that rather than placing the focus on angels, it was always best to keep the focus on the organization (or the individual) becoming a channel of the Creator, a channel of understanding the connectedness of all of humankind, and a channel of the awareness of our ultimate oneness with all of Creation. By keeping the focus in this direction, the Divine would send the angelic forces when they were needed.

Maintaining an appropriate spiritual ideal and focusing on an appropriate tone that would best facilitate spiritual guidance were also outlined in a reading given to a member of the Quaker faith when she sought past-life information and guidance for herself; Cayce described it in this way:

> First, know what is thy ideal. In whom have you put your trust? What are His promises to thee? How many, how much do you make those promises thine? For what purpose do ye strive with material things in this material experience? Is it for the glory of an idea, or for the glory of thy ideal? or is it merely to satisfy self?
>
> Answer these questions within thine own conscience. And do not take them lightly. For they are the basis of thy philosophy, they are the questions ye must answer before thine own guardian angel that stands ever before the face of Him as is thyself!
> 1620-2

The readings also indicate that an angel's dedication to an individual's personal growth and development may cross over to more than one lifetime, if not all lifetimes. One example can be found in a life reading given to an eleven-year-old girl whose parents had sought

Cayce's counsel as a way of determining the best school to send their daughter to as well as a means of understanding what direction her talents and abilities would eventually take. The information stated that she had innate talents in music and drama and that her training should encompass both because she might ultimately decide to choose a career in the motion picture industry. For this individual, as well as for all others, the reading reminded the parents of the important role spirituality should play in her life: " . . . find first self—and self's relationships to the Creative influences that are manifested in a material world. *Know* in whom, in what, self believes, as related to the spiritual life, in the application of self . . . " (405-1)

The reading went on to describe several past lives that were having an influence upon the present, including one as a Jamestown settler, when she had known both of her parents, as well as one in which she had been the wife of the Roman soldier who had stood by the cross during the crucifixion. Her reading described that lifetime, as follows:

> The entity then was the companion of, the wife of, that soldier that stood by the Cross when the Son of man was put thereon; in the name Marcellus.
>
> Through this experience the entity gained and gained. While the positions in the social life of the entity made for associations with those of the royalty and with those that were persecuted, even that were given to the lions in that experience, the entity held self rather in that position as being able to give help both to those persecuted and strength to those whom duty demanded oft to act in the capacity of the persecutors.   405-1

When it came time for questions, the girl asked Mr. Cayce, "Do I have a guide, or guides, in the spirit world or plane?" The answer not only confirmed the presence of the guardian angel that had apparently been involved with the girl for at least 2,000 years, but a follow-up question once again confirmed that the capacity of angelic help and guidance was connected to each individual's own commitment to a spiritual path. The answer came:

There are ever, for every soul, those that may be termed the guides or guardian angels that stand before the throne of grace and mercy. The guardian angel for this entity (as may be termed) is that one, Aruel, who stood with Marcellus at the Cross.

The next question was, "Will I be able to have protection and guidance from the spirit plane to help me carry out my ideals for my best development in this life?" Cayce responded: "If there is the finding of self in its relationships to the spiritual life, and the guiding of self therein; as given. Then do the angels and the guards in the spiritual life protect those in their activities."

When a fifty-seven-year-old man obtained a reading, part of his impetus was an attempt to understand why he had such an affinity for things of both a psychic and a spiritual nature. He was also drawn to spiritual healing and the energy of prayer. Edgar Cayce told him that it was more than simply a passing interest or an attraction. In fact, when the man inquired what level of "degree" he actually possessed these talents, the reading responded that they were innate abilities and had been mastered in previous incarnations: "The abilities to heal, the abilities to teach, the abilities to minister, *all* are thine! As to degrees—to the nth; yea, to the tenth degree may they be manifest in thee!" (707-1) One of those incarnations had been a lifetime just previous to the present when he had been a revered medicine man for a Native American tribe in the area now known as Talladega, Alabama.

In spite of the encouragement provided by the reading, however, the individual was apparently hesitant to pursue his spiritual interests. Whether it was personal insecurity or concern about whether or not his talents were real, the gentleman retained some measure of doubt and fear. In response, Cayce counseled him that as long as he trusted in God, divine guidance was ever-present and even the angelic realms would be there to assist him:

…"If ye will be my son, I will be thy Father-God. If ye will trust in me, I will not forsake thee." Though the heavens may fall, though the earth may pass away, thy spirit and thy faith in Him will *not* be shaken, for He abides with thee and hath given His angels charge concerning thee lest thou, in thy fury, in thine self, dash thine head, thine foot, against the stone.   707-1

Follow-up notations in Mr. [707]'s file confirm that he pursued his interest in healing. He later married a woman with some of the same interests. He also told other people that his reading had given him the encouragement and "a sense of freedom" that he was, in fact, doing God's will. One of the notations citing Mr. [707]'s efficacy with prayer is as follows:

> A few weeks ago a man was arrested here [New York] because his car was throwing off a volume of smoke, and was to appear at Court the next morning. That night Mr. [707] prayed for the man, and when the man went to Court the next morning the Judge said the case had been thrown out of Court.
>
> Report 707-2

A similar challenge with fear and insecurity was described by a fifty-two-year-old woman who complained about "mental distress and worry." The woman admitted that these ongoing thoughts were causing her to feel like she was "at war with herself." Her reading stated that these feelings were being created because there was an incoordination between the part of her thought processes that were interested in pursuing her spiritual ideals and that part of her mind that seemed to dwell on "self-condemnation." When she wondered aloud why she so often had issues with physical suffering and mental worry, the response was that it was due to fear within herself. Once again, the readings encouraged her to become cognizant of the fact that there were spiritual elements that were standing ready to assist her even in the face of her fears:

> ...Fear is as the fruit of indecisions respecting that which is lived and that which is held as the ideal. Doubt is as the father of fear. Remember, as He gave, "He that asks in my name, doubting not, shall have; for I go to the Father." If doubt has crept in, it becomes as the father of fear. Fear is as the beginning of faltering. Faltering is as that which makes for dis-ease throughout the soul and mental body . . . "He—God—is One," and making self in an at-onement, is not only *denying* any other influence but acting in the way knowing that He will bear thee up—and give

His angels charge concerning thee in the way thou goest, lest thou dash thine self against a barrier. Then, when there arises those experiences where *fear* comes from faltering in self or another, *force* self—by *will*—"I *will!*"—to give, live and *know* that He doeth all things *well* in and through the expression of the Father in every soul! Then may the body in the present, the body-consciousness, the mental-consciousness, have that peace that passeth understanding, that comes from an at-one-ment in the consciousness of His love dwelling within. 538-33

The presence of a guardian angel intervening to help an individual overcome personal fears was cited in a reading given to a thirty–three–year–old college student who had been on the battlefield in his present life during the later portion of World War I (1914–1918). The young man had been around only twenty at the time, obviously very much afraid, when quite suddenly he found the courage and conviction from within to continue his march on the field. That courage had apparently come from the angelic realm for Cayce described what had happened, as follows: " . . . the guardian angel stooped down to quell those fears that arose in the entity's self . . . " (1909-1) In a follow–up reading, the student asked for additional details; Cayce provided the following:

. . . In the angel stopping on the field . . . the entity was being guided, or guarded, or protected, that that as had been prom-ised from the foundations of the world would be to each indi-vidual, "If ye will be my people I will be thy God." He that walketh is the light, and purposes in his heart to *do*, *be*, that which *the* Creative Forces would *have* one be, shall *not* be *left* alone! . . .
1909-3

In another instance, Cayce suggested that the spiritual realm was trying to assist a fifty–seven–year old executive, but his own depression and fear were apparently cutting off the very help that was trying to come to him. Not deeply interested in things of a spiritual nature, his focus had generally been turned to the financial world. Unfortunately, due to some bad business decisions and the Depression, the executive had lost his business and a great deal of money. In his despair, he wrote a suicide note for his wife and children and then disappeared. The family requested several readings from Edgar Cayce to discern whether he was still alive, and, if so, to help find him. Apparently, the man's intense fear and hopelessness made it impossible for even Edgar Cayce to discern his location, for although the reading confirmed he was still alive, when tuning into the individual Cayce stated, "*Where* is this? Where is this? What is this about the body that hinders so; that surrounds in such a maze that keeps aid from coming?" The reading continued:

> When thou hast chosen those things that block the way for the greatness of the spirit of light to enter, thou makest the way hard even for those that would do thee good. Thou shuttest them out from thine companionship. Thou cuttest them off from being that help and aid that makes for the light that would guide thee.   378-27

In an effort to help her husband overcome his despair, the wife and her children were encouraged to pray for him — to see him surrounding by light. The spiritual energy they provided would surround him and assist the spirit in rendering aid. Toward the end of the reading, Edgar Cayce confirmed that the individual was still alive ("still in body") but even the sleeping Cayce was still unable to discern the man's location: "Where is this? *Where?*" Apparently giving advice for both the executive and the family, the reading ended with the encouragement that the angelic realms could intervene to banish his fears and eliminate the "walls of darkness" that still filled his mind:

> …Make known unto the Lord what thou wouldst do. The mind will clear in Him. Hold tight to that faith thou hast in Him that is able to keep that thou committest unto Him, for in His arms He will bear thee up—and He will give His angels charge concerning thee. They will banish those fears, those walls of darkness that thou hast built in thine determinations, in thine recklessness in mind. For, savourest thou of the things that take hold onto those things that bring fear and darkness, thou turnest thy face from the light.   378-27

Unbeknownst to Edgar Cayce or the man's family at the time, the executive was essentially wandering the country, deeply troubled about his loss and the mistakes he had made. His journey would last months. Throughout that time, the family continued their prayers. Perhaps confirming the readings' conviction that angelic intercession could sometimes come through as a hunch or a thought, somewhere along the way the executive came across a book by Emmet Fox, a New Thought spiritual leader, which seemed to be the transformation that he needed to turn his life around. Five months after his initial disappearance, his wife wrote a letter to the Cayce office enclosing a letter from her husband. The woman suggested that her husband's letter demonstrated that he had actually found a passion for things of a spiritual nature; she stated that his letter "will surprise you, as much as it did me. The letter is a holy thing, it shows the birth of a soul and, as such, I hope it will prove a great blessing in some way to you." His correspondence follows:

> Some 5 months ago my affairs seemed so hopeless, the tangle so muddled, that I could not see my way out. Now, thanks to the books by Emmet Fox . . . and the deep understanding and love of my good wife, everything is changing completely. It is a real miracle to watch how God is unfolding for us a glorious and wonderful plan for a happy new career, and all through scientific prayer. Almost each day some new development is bringing us nearer to our ultimate goal of establishing a happy home, where I can be actively engaged in business, applying the principles that I have absorbed by being guided into the path of right thoughts . . . Had I known what I know today, everything would be different. I had been living in a Fool's Paradise and needed this shock to cleanse my soul . . .   Report 378-50

In addition to the possibility of seeing angels or just knowing that they are always in attendance, the readings suggest that there are experiences that can confirm their presence. For example, when a member of a prayer group spoke about an experience she had while meditating, Cayce stated that it had occurred because she had been in the presence of an angel. She had voiced the following: "On several occasions while meditating with the group there was a cool feeling as if mentholatum

had been placed upon my head and forehead, extending down upon
the nose." Cayce replied:

> As would be termed—literal—as the breath of an angel, or the
> breath of a master. As the body attunes self, as has been given,
> it may be a channel where there may be even *instant* healing
> with the laying on of hands. The more often this occurs the
> more *power* is there felt in the body, the forcefulness in the act
> or word.   281-5

The readings indicate that the angelic realms are essentially the spiritual manifestation of the Creator in the earth. Their role is to provide
an aiding influence, guidance, and even knowledge for individuals in
their mental and spiritual development. In one reading, these angelic
beings are described as "the laws of the universe," (5749-3) but the readings make it clear that their involvement in the lives of individuals is
conditioned by that person's openness and commitment to his or her
true spiritual self.

As one example, during a reading given to a retired bank executive,
while discussing this spiritual importance Cayce used the following
terminology: "He has entrusted to mankind . . . [so] it behooves each
individual—as the body so oft finds—to be up and doing that which
the hands find to do." The reading went on to state that "each soul enters with a mission." As the individual attempts to apply that mission,
which always has something to do with providing help and assistance
to others, that individual can be guided and assisted by the spiritual
realms. Personal choice and will apparently open the door to angelic
assistance. In the language of the readings, the banker was told: " . . . for
indeed the guardian angel is ever before the throne of grace for each
and every soul . . . by purpose of the individual self *as* it has applied
and does apply that concept, that ideal which is chosen through each
activity of the entity. (1662-2)

On another occasion, a real estate broker had a series of health readings. He had problems with his liver and kidneys. He also had anemia
and poor circulation. Over time, Cayce recommended a number of
therapies include osteopathy, massage, prescription medication, and
working with spiritual ideals and things of a spiritual nature. During

the course of his reading, the individual asked about whether or not his guardian angel could assist him as a "healing force for physical betterment." Edgar Cayce replied:

> The guardian angel—that is the companion of each soul as it enters into a material experience—is ever an influence for the keeping of that attunement between the creative energies or forces of the soul-entity *and* health, life, light and immortality. Thus, to be sure, it is a portion of that influence for *healing* forces. And as may be experienced in the activities of individuals, it may become so accentuated as to be the greater influence in their experience ...
> 1646-1

The reading went on to confirm that just as it was necessary to make physical adjustments to become healthier, it was just as important to make adjustments that would promote "the spiritual and mental self" becoming more in attunement to the spirit within. In fact, the "guardian force" that could render assistance to him was conditional upon his purpose, desire, will, and attunement striving to gain an awareness of his oneness with God. When the individual asked whether it was "through the guardian angel that God speaks to the individual?", the reading gave a surprising response, suggesting that the individual's own Higher Self (or spirit self) was in such attunement to the guardian angel that they were one and the same!

> Then as the guardian influence or angel is ever before the face of the Father, through same may that influence ever speak—but only by the command of or attunement to that which is thy ideal. What then is thy ideal? In *whom* have ye believed, as well as in what have ye believed? Is that in which thou hast believed able to keep ever before thee that thou committest unto Him? Yes—through thy angel, through thy *self* that *is* the angel— does the self speak with thy Ideal!
> 1646-1

On other occasions, however, the readings repeatedly confirm that angels are a separate form of Creation from human beings and that humans have the ability to become one with God. For example, when an individual asked for additional information about the human capacity to exercise free will and whether or not God intended humankind to use that will with the hope that it would return to the divine, Cayce responded:

> . . . As has been given, man was made a little lower than the angels, yet with that power to become one with God, while the angel remains the angel. In the life, then, of Jesus we find the oneness made manifest through the ability to overcome all of the temptations of the flesh, and the desires of same, through making the *will one with the Father*. For as we find, oft did He give to those about Him those injunctions, "Those who have seen me have seen the Father," and in man, He, the Son of Man, became one with the Father. Man, through the same channel, may reach that perfection, even higher than the angel, though he attend the God.   900-16

This premise is repeated in a number of places throughout the readings, such as the following:

> For a man is a little lower than the angels, yet was made that he might become the companion of the Creative Forces; and thus was given—in the breath of life—the individual soul, the stamp of approval as it were of the Creator; with the ability to know itself to be itself, and to make itself, as one with the Creative Forces—*irrespective* of other influences.   1456-1

> For he, man, has been made just a little lower than the angels; with all the abilities to become *one with Him!* not the whole, nor yet lost in the individuality of the whole, but becoming more and more personal in *all* of its consciousnesses of the application of the individuality of Creative Forces, thus more and more at-onement with Him—yet conscious of being himself. 2172-1

Another statement regarding angels that is frequently repeated in the Cayce material comes from Hebrews 13:2, where it states: "Be not forgetful to entertain strangers: for thereby some have entertained angels unawares." Obviously, the statement suggests that there are times when individuals do not realize they are in the presence of angels. Although unfortunately not providing additional details, on one occasion Edgar Cayce himself confirmed to a client that he had experienced seeing angels firsthand. A fifty-year-old sales engineer wrote Mr. Cayce to tell him about a dream. Cayce's response was to remind the individual that God often spoke to us in our dreams. The same letter confirmed Cayce's experience with angels:

> …God in olden times appeared, not only to the leaders and the rulers, but to the laymen, in visions and in dreams. When our soul body goes out in sleep or when the consciousness of the physical is laid aside, the soul consciousness may become easily attuned with that which we have attuned our souls with or that we think on, for mind is still the builder, and it is not presumptuous, I don't think, to say that oftentimes we have angels visit us unawares. I have seen them. It is that we do not consider them or take stock of ourselves as to that we have been thinking, dreaming, or speaking. When we do, it is often not very hard to make such a connection that it is found to be worth while.
>
> Report 333-3

In addition to angels, the Cayce readings confirm the existence of a group of spiritual adepts who have apparently completed their spiritual progression in the earth and—much like the angelic realms—remain as an energetic group of spiritual helpers assisting humankind along the way. Although these adepts could have been male or female in their most recent incarnation and come from every imaginable religious background, culture, race, and point in history, Cayce referred to them as the "White Brotherhood." The title apparently designating both the intenseness of the white light that surrounds them as well as the collective goal they hold with one another. On a number of occasions, Edgar Cayce met some of these individuals who appeared to him. With all of this as background information, on one occasion a sixty-eight-year-old medical doctor inquired: "Is it likely that I will meet any of the brothers [White Brotherhood] in the flesh, as Mr. Cayce has done, in this incarnation? If so, where and when?" The response came: "Ye may meet many. For, oft doth man entertain angels unawares." (3011–3)

Similar advice, confirming the existence of these spiritual beings that often interacted with humans without their awareness was given to a sixty–seven–year–old composer during the course of her reading. Although possessing many strengths in art and music, she apparently had issues with hate, jealousy, and fear, and sometimes considered certain people as not being worth her time or attention. The reading's counsel was as follows:

> Thus it behooves the entity, in the present, not only to study to show self aware but capable of giving proper evaluations as to needs in the mental, the spiritual and the material experience of dealing with the fellow man. For with what measure you mete, it is measured to thee again … Then, in same, heed that injunction which may be a part of self: Be not unmindful to entertain those even who may appear not physically, mentally or materially necessary in thy experience. For many have entertained angels unaware …   2131-1

One of the things that the readings often suggested for couples was to find a oneness of purpose that they could always agree on in their relationship. In other words, when times became challenging or when there was conflict between them, what was the core purpose of their relationship that they could always agree upon? With this in mind, when a young woman came to Edgar Cayce for advice prior to marrying her fiancé and asked, "What is our greatest purpose together in this life?" Cayce's reply was simple: "Harmony!" The reading went on to suggest that it was possible to create such a positive energetic vibration in relationships that it would attract the angelic realms. His advice for their marriage was as follows:

> In the establishing of the home, make it as that which may be the pattern of a heavenly home. Not as that set aside for only a place to sleep or to rest, but where not only self but all who enter there may feel, may experience, by the very vibrations that are set up by each in the sacredness of the home, a helpfulness, a *hopefulness* in the air *about* the home. As not only a place of

rest, not only a place of recreation for the mind, not only a place
as a haven for the bodies and minds of both but for all that may
be as visitors or as guests. And remember those injunctions that
have been in thine experience in many of thine sojourns, and be
thou mindful of the entertaining of the guests; for some have
entertained angels unawares. Make thine home, thine abode,
where an angel would *desire* to visit, where an angel would seek
to be a guest. For it will bring the greater blessings, the greater
glories, the greater contentment, the greater satisfaction; the
glorious harmony of adjusting thyself and thy relationships one
with another in making same ever harmonious. Do not begin
with, "We will do it tomorrow—we will begin next week—we
will make for such next year." Let that thou sowest in thy relationships day by day be the seeds of truth, of hope, that as they
grow to fruition in thy relationships, as the days and the months
and the years that are to come go by, they will grow into that
garden of beauty that makes indeed for the home.   480-20

A young woman whose family was extremely interested in the Edgar
Cayce work received numerous readings over a period of eight years.
During one of her life readings, she was told that she possessed innate
talents with music, apparently connected with her work in one of the
healing temples during a past life in Egypt. She was advised that her
talent could best be demonstrated through her playing the harp. Her
other interests included art, writing, nutrition, and spirit guides, and on
one occasion she asked for the name of her spirit guide. The reading
advised that every individual had a guide that was "before the throne"
but for her own spiritual development her focus should be on her inner
self not an external guide. (275-31)

At a later time, the young woman learned that in her Egyptian life
she had been adept at assisting individuals in their own spiritual development because of her skills as a musician. That talent was something she could use once again—not only for others but for herself. The
reading stated: " . . . the music and that which arises with same will not
only create or build experiences in the entity's own activities that will
make for the renewing of self from within, but the ability to give out to
others that which will enable them—as individuals, as souls—to seek to

know their relationships with the Creative influences . . . " She asked, "Give more detailed help *now* as to how I can come in attunement with my inner self through music?" and Cayce replied:

> In the practice periods (which in the material world are necessary, to acquaint self with the action of the spiritual influences from within, to arouse all forms or forces of the mental influences that would radiate through the activities of materiality) study in self not mere form, but the spirit of the form in movement, in the activity of that which makes for the practice periods. See, through the intuitive self, the spirit of that which *impelled* the recorder of the notes or the music, and there is aroused in self then that which will make for periods when not of self but rather as of angels in the seraphim choir will be the activity; rather as of the spirit of truth. For, know ye well that the Prince of Peace was a harpist Himself! In the meditation, then, make thy actions rather such as might be guided by Him; and the influence and the activities, and that which it brings to self and that which it gives out and creates in the hearts, minds, and souls of others, will be *spiritual*—and spiritual uplift—and aiding to all of the emotional influences in the activities of individuals, as to bring *healing,* harmony, joy, peace, love, in the experience of the hearers   275-35

In subsequent readings the same woman was told that during her meditations to imagine herself surrounded " . . . with that consciousness of His angels having been given charge concerning thee." (275–36) She was also advised that there were few individuals in the earth who could attune to and work with spiritual energy in her own work as she could. (275–37) Over the years she became extremely adept with the harp. Cayce told her that her music enabled herself to attune to the "realms of the infinite." Eventually, she became a member of an orchestra and a well-known musician playing background music with her harp. Her music seemed to possess the ability to bring spirit into the earth, and one occasion a reading suggested that her talent was such that the angels themselves would "stoop down to listen":

Hence in seeking in self for those varied influences that may bring joy or peace or harmony, as does music into the ears of those that may hear ... And thus does it raise the soul and the heart to that rhythm, that harmony, that makes for joy—even in heaven. For, as it—such harmony, such music as may this entity raise in its own activity, bring even joy at the Throne. And in those heavenly places where the angels stoop down to listen, and the harkening of those that would bring into the souls and hearts of men a strengthening—by those that may play even as this entity. Then, knowing that such is, to whom and how may it enter to gain the more? Opening self as in the meditation, and then *pray* as He guides thy fingers, thy hands, thine body!

275-39

Although confirming that angels are ever-present in people's lives, on a number of occasions individuals were told how their spiritual endeavors had evoked the help of the angels. For example, a woman's grown nephew had apparently been ill and died in his own apartment. The woman asked what help he had received during his transition. Cayce replied that the help had come from his own guardian angel, prompted, in part, by the woman's prayers and concerns. The woman admitted that she felt her nephew's presence a few days later in her apartment, and she wanted to know whether or not the experience had been real. The reading confirmed that he had, in fact, been in her apartment at that very moment. (1472-4)

Acting in a manner that would place a focus on spiritual development was the approach suggested for opening self to the presence and aid of the angelic realms. This was the advice given to an electrical engineering student who was apparently too often laid back and fond of the motto, "Let's see what will happen." Cayce counseled that this approach was not very helpful in terms of his own growth and development and had actually created an issue in which "there has not been kept as perfect a record of the activities as there should be . . . " (440-14) It was recommended that he use more focus and concentrated effort in his endeavors. He was encouraged to think about his soul self and ponder the question: "is the soul seeking for expression that it may satisfy its *own* personality? or for the glory of the individuality that is of God?"

He was advised to always use what he had in hand, to go out of his way to be of service to others, and to know that as long as he sought the Divine he would be shown the way. Cayce added:

> ... For, above all, keep thy *balance*, in spirit, in truth, in body, in mind, as has been given thee; else thou may lose thy way! But put thyself in that position where He may give His angels charge concerning thee, and never "Let's see what will happen."
>
> 440-14

A couple in their thirties obtained a reading on how they could best build a life together and both fulfill the purpose for which they had come into the earth at this time. During the course of the reading, Cayce advised that in order to fulfill what they were asking, they should pray the same prayer several times each day at the same time, even when they were not together, as follows:

> Then, let the prayer of each be—three times each day—agree upon a time—not merely say it, but feel it, be it: *"Lord! Thy will be done in me, today. Lord, Thy will be done in me today."* Then, as ye go about thy daily tasks, in associations with others, let thy words, thy acts, thy thoughts, be ever, *"Lord, Thy will be done in me today."* This does not mean that there is to be long-facedness, but joy—even as in Him when He wept with those that wept and rejoiced with those that did rejoice; even supplying the wine, even of greater flavor and potency than the bridegroom was able to supply. He was *all* things to all men. *Ye,* under His direction, by that constant prayer, may be—daily—all things to all men. Thus will each soul be *glad,* be *joyous,* in thy coming, and sorrow at thy going.
>
> 2533-7

When the husband asked how he and his wife could enlist the aid of the angels in their life together, Cayce stated that by saying the prayer: *"Lord, Thy will be done in me today,"* God would dispatch the angelic realms to be concerned with them both:

> Every experience is an assurance. And as He has given, Behold

the face of the angels ever stands before the throne of God; the awareness in self that thou may be one with, equal with, the Father-God, as His child, as the brother of the Christ, thy Savior, thy Brother. And as the awareness comes, it is as the angel of hope, the angel of announcing, the angel of declaiming, the angel that would warn, the angel that would protect. For, these are ever as awarenesses, as consciousnesses of the abiding presence ...

Taken together the Edgar Cayce readings are extremely clear in the conviction that the angelic realms surround all of humankind. Their role is to assist each and every individual in fulfilling that purpose for which he or she came into the earth. They serve as a source of guidance and inspiration that may come in a dream, in a hunch, in a chance encounter, or in a book or a song that "just happens" to come our way. Ultimately, their role is to help individuals grow toward at-one-ment with the Divine. They stand ever ready and are called into action by our thoughts and activities. Cayce stated that the choices we make toward personal development evokes such an energetic power that it can shine like " ... a new star in the universe ... " (1695–1), apparently becoming a beacon for others to see. And the angels are always there to assist us, for as Edgar Cayce often reassured individuals, "God is mindful of thee."

2

Spirit Guides and Other Angelic Beings

In addition to the ongoing influence of angels, the Edgar Cayce readings repeatedly confirmed the existence of a variety of spirit guides whose role is that of helping individuals in their journey through life. These guides not only come from various levels of the angelic realms and include all manner of energetic beings ranging from other angels to what Cayce referred to as "elementals," but they also include the influence and guidance of dead relatives and deceased friends who have crossed to the "other side" and generally aim to serve as a helpful influence. From Cayce's perspective, the assistance of spirit guides can come in the form of direct communication, psychic information, a sudden hunch that seems to come from nowhere, and from information in dreams. Each of these approaches enables the subconscious mind of the individual to communicate with the consciousness of the spirit guide. What may be somewhat unique about the Cayce approach to these guides is that he repeatedly confirmed their existence but at the same time counseled individuals not to seek them outright. Once again, the readings advised individuals to seek only the presence of God or the Christ spirit, which would enable these guides to be used and have an influence only when it was in the best interest of self.

On one occasion when a forty–one–year–old woman sought personal advice on spiritual guidance, Cayce encouraged her to seek the highest source as "the infinite is much greater" than any guide she might contact. He also added that just as she was on her own path of development, any guide she might be influenced by would have personal limitations of its own:

> . . . *Do not* allow this to be directed by an entity that does proclaim himself or herself as *being* the guide. Why? For, as indicated, the abilities have been such in self—and the soul development—that to call upon the Infinite is much greater, much more satisfying, much more worth while in the experience of an individual soul than being guided or directed merely by an entity outside of self that—*as* self—*is* being in a state of transition or development. There may be experiences when individual entities may proclaim or indicate their own activity by a name, but—as has ever been proclaimed—a name immediately sets metes and bounds about the abilities or the experience of development for a given period. Not that (as a very crude example) one would send for a plumber to judge a painting. One would not seek a well-digger to judge a musical interpretation. One would not seek for those merely because they had experienced a view without the development or training. But, as God's purpose is to *glorify* the individual man (or soul) in the earth, so the highest purpose of an individual soul or entity is to glorify the Creative Energy or God in the earth. Should the Maker use a gnome, a fairy, an angel, a developing entity *for* a guide, alright—for a specific direction; for He hath given His angels charge concerning thee, and *thy* god, thy face, is ever before the Throne of the Infinite.   338-3

Similar advice was given to a fifty–five–year–old woman who was often putting herself in an altered state of consciousness which opened her up psychically to the awareness of other entities in the spirit realm.

Cayce asked her, "Why trust entities not any more endowed with spirituality than self?" Apparently, her propensity of attuning to other levels
of consciousness could be traced to a lifetime in ancient Egypt when she
had been able to do the very same thing. Rather than relying upon the
information from these spirits and lesser guides, she was encouraged to
explore scripture, including John 14–17, and to gain an understanding
of the words Jesus spoke: "In my Father's house are many mansions"
(many levels of consciousness and states of awareness). In terms of what
she could ultimately learn from these higher levels of consciousness,
Cayce's counseled:

> Thus study thyself, and know thy ideals; that ye may walk in the
> straight and the narrow way.
>   But do write at times of thy own experiences, rather than of
> those that would enslave thee in their own weaknesses. For, He
> has promised to be with those that seek His biddings. Know He
> is not far from thee, daily.
>   Let thy light so shine that others, seeing, may take hope, and
> may walk the closer with the Creative Force, God.   3000-2

The importance of having ideals was also stressed in a reading given
to a lab technician who was extremely psychic. Apparently sensitive to
visions of both elementals and angels, the woman knew that the name
of one of her guides was Abdulla. When she asked whether or not
Abdulla was a worthy guide for her "to work with," Cayce's response
connected the answer to her own spiritual ideal: "Only when such
influences are kept in accord with your own ideal are they worthy;
but keep thine own ideal! For each soul must answer to self and the
consciousness within!" (1387–1)

In 1934, a prominent socialite who was well versed in Theosophy as
well as Eastern and Western religious traditions sought a reading on
how she could continue to develop her own psychic abilities specifically for her "higher spiritual development." As part of that process, she
wondered whether she should pursue writing a book personally or instead attempt to channel one through trance mediumship. The reading
advised her that by writing it personally she would contribute much
more to her own soul growth and development because she would be

accessing the consciousness of her higher self rather than attempting to contact something outside of herself. When she asked how to make decisions that were more in keeping with a spiritual ideal rather than the events or circumstances of the moment, Cayce provided the following:

> ... First seek an answer consciously for any question within thine own environ, thine own surroundings, and let thine own development, thine own ideas, answer yes or no. Then take the answer—yes or no—to the inner consciousness [such as in meditation] and let thy ruling influence in the Spirit answer. And ye may know, and the truth in same sets you free ... Let the answer be in the highest—mental, and then in the spirit itself from within.   443-3

She also asked about spirit guides and Cayce confirmed that every individual has guides. He went on to suggest that the level of a guide was interconnected with an individual's own soul development and the choices that the individual was making in life. In other words, the higher a person's level of spiritual attainment, the higher would be the level of guides and angels that the individual drew to himself or herself. The reading added that just because a guide was in the spirit plane, it was important to remember that " . . . all are not teachers, all are not ministers, all are not healers . . . " They have their own talents, abilities, and shortcoming, just as those in the material world. It was in the process of choosing the path of spirit that individuals opened themselves to the highest form of guidance and protection. In the language of the readings: " . . . each soul *has* an individual guide—but the more often does such rise or develop by the choosing. As has been given, 'There is set before thee life and death, good and evil—choose thou.' But it is just as true, 'His angels have been given charge concerning thee . . . '" Because of her personal development she could have access to as high a source as desired, but she was encouraged to seek the "cosmic or universal [God] sources."

Another couple who had readings from Edgar Cayce was extremely interested in spirit guides and spirit communication. In his most recent past life, the husband had apparently been a Nordic adventurer and seafarer with an intense interest in Norse mythology and the ways in which the gods could communicate with humankind. (2124-3) That lifetime may have been the impetus for his intense interest in spirit communication in the present. The wife was told that as a young girl in one of her previous incarnations she had been among the shepherds on the hillside of Bethlehem and had heard firsthand the angelic choir announcing the birth of Jesus. This experience may have been at the heart of her firm belief that it was it was truly possible to speak to guides and the spirit realm. (2125-1)

The wife also stated that she often heard the name "Abercrombie," as though it were being whispered in her mind. When she asked about the name, Cayce confirmed that it was a guide she had been associated with and continued to be connected to her because of her involvement in spiritualism. On another occasion, she sought information on how she might work with "automatic writing," apparently in an effort to communicate more clearly with Abercrombie. The answer was that anyone could develop automatic writing, but a more important question might be whether or not there were better ways to attune to the spiritual realms. In fact, when she asked, "Who is giving me this message?" The response came, "That one sought from," suggesting that it was Abercrombie himself that was cautioning her against the practice. (262-25)

A series of readings that confirmed the ongoing presence of spirit guides occurred in the case of a commercial agent for the railroad. He had a series of readings between 1930 and 1933, a number of which mentioned that the guide was present and several confirming how the individual had been connected to the guide previously. For example, during the course of a reading in which an answer was given detailing how the commercial agent might change his work environment, the individual asked, "Who is giving the information?" The reply came, "Demetrius." When the commercial agent asked whether he could call on this guide for help and guidance in the future, the reply came: "This, my brother, is much to be asked—even of me, thine own brother in the flesh . . . that same may oft become a stumbling block to thine own self . . . " (311-5) This and subsequent readings suggested that it was not a good idea to seek help from Demetrius directly; instead, it seemed that Demetrius would make an appearance when the higher forces felt his presence might be helpful The readings would eventually confirm that Demetrius had been the brother of the commercial agent on at least two previous occasions—once in Palestine and once in Egypt.

During a follow-up reading that recommended the individual stay with the railroad industry but perhaps change his place of employment to Newark and focus more on labor, again the agent asked, "Who is giving this information?" And the response came, "There has been given that one who seeks to aid in directing. Demetrius." (311-7)

During a reading that focused on negotiations with the Norfolk Southern railroad, after Cayce had given a brief discussion, Demetrius seemed to interject with the following: "For the moment, then, Demetrius would philosophize on the situations—for the moment." (311-8)

And finally, in 1933 when the commercial agent asked for insights into whom to approach about a possible position with the Southern Railway in Washington, DC, after the information was given, the spirit guide identified himself once again as "Demetrius." (311-12)

One of the most interesting examples of ongoing communication with a spirit guide is the case of a young woman named Rose[15] who had a series of readings over a four-year-period that explored some of the guidance and advice she was getting from her deceased mother in the spirit realm. Although only in her sixties, her mother had died due to atherosclerosis and complications from a stroke and a blood clot behind her eyes. Rose and her mother, Lucille, had been very close, and after her death Lucille apparently took on the role of a frequent guide and counselor, remaining very concerned about her daughter's life.

Perhaps because of Rose's psychic sensitivity, on occasion other deceased friends and relatives made an appearance as guides, as well. One of the earliest communications was from an older woman Rose called "J.S." who had cared for her when she had been a child. Rose had not seen J.S. in several years but knew that the older woman had died three weeks before her own mother. One night while Rose was sleeping, still very much grieving at her mother's passing, J.S. came to her in a dream and assured her in a strong voice: *"Your mother is as happy as ever."* When she asked about the dream in a Cayce reading, Cayce confirmed that it was real communication from J.S., who was trying to comfort her. The reading also counseled her that she should be reassured that her mother was just fine and continued to love and be aware of her:

---

[15]The name has been changed for confidentiality; case #136.

... Then, the entity should gain that strength from that given regarding the condition, and know that the mother lives in that realm in which there is recognized J.S. and that the companionship is there, until those developments come from the earth plane to lead on to those higher realms, or to come again. For those many changes must come to each and every entity in its development. And as these are seen, then, the strength, the understanding, should be gained by this entity. For as is given, she is *well*, *happy*, and *free* from the care as is given in earth's plane, yet with that same love as is raised through the companionship with the oneness of the spiritual forces with the soul, see?

136-33

During the course of the reading, Rose stated that she had not even been thinking about J.S. and she wondered, "how and why did this entity [J.S.] transmit the message to me?" In response, Cayce suggested that she could have received the information directly from her mother but that her own deep sorrow and "self–condemnation" over some of the events dealing with her mother's care and passing were apparently blocking the communication. Some of the dialogue between the sleep–ing Cayce and Rose present in the room for the reading follows:

(Q) Was J.S. there to guide Mother over the transition from physical to spiritual? Both died within 3 weeks—both must easily have yet been—be in this plane as yet—is this so?
(A) Both in physical plane or earth's sphere as yet, until that force leads on in its ever developing toward that Oneness with the All Force, see?
(Q) Then, does one spirit guide another over?
(A) "Lo! I am with thee, and though I walk through the valley of the shadow of death, my spirit shall guide thee ..."
(Q) Voice: "Your Mother is alive and happy."
(A) Your mother is alive and happy ... for there is no death, only the transition from the physical to the spiritual plane. Then, as the birth into the physical is given as the time of the new life, just so, then, in physical is the birth into the spiritual.
(Q) Then, does my mother see me and love me as ever?

(A) Sees thee and loves thee as ever. Just as those forces were manifest in the physical world, and the entity entertains and desires and places self in that attunement with those desires of that entity, the love exists, in that far, in that manner, see? for in spirit all sham is laid aside.

(Q) Does she try to tell me "I am alive and happy?"

(A) *Tells* the entity "I am alive and happy" when entity will *attune* self to that at-oneness ... for the *soul* liveth, and is at peace, and would that this entity know that it liveth. And as has been given, "In my Father's house are many mansions, were it not so I would have told you," and "I go to prepare a place for you, that where *I am* there *ye* may be also ..." let this be as the *lesson* to the entity: If the filial love is shown in the *material* world in such a manner, how much *greater* must be that love expressed by the Father in Heaven!   136-33

Shortly after the communication, Rose became pregnant with her first child. She and her husband, Edward, were extremely excited about having a baby. Unfortunately, within the first few months Rose had a miscarriage. The couple wanted to try again, but before becoming pregnant a second time, Rose had a dream about her mother. In the dream, her mother said that she was concerned about Rose's health and so the mother decided to contact a doctor to be of assistance. Later, during a reading, Rose asked Edgar Cayce about the dream, and he informed her that it had been a real communication between her and Lucille and that her mother continued to be concerned about her physical and mental health. If Rose wanted to have a successful pregnancy, she needed to prepare herself " . . . mentally and physically for that conceptive condition which should take place in the present year..." (136–36)

A few months later, Rose apparently complained to her husband about ongoing back problems. Edward encouraged her to see an osteopath; she refused. The back pains continued, but Rose did not want to go to another physician. Again, her husband encouraged her to go to an osteopath, but she ignored him. He was frustrated that she would not listen to what he thought was helpful advice. Rose later found out that he began praying to Lucille, his deceased mother–in–law, to convince her daughter to go to the doctor. One night, Rose had a dream:

"Morning of August 17. My mother appeared to me. I saw her very distinctly. She said to me: 'You should go to the osteopath. You ought to be ashamed of yourself! If Edward wants you to go to the osteopath, you should go.'"

When Rose asked Edgar Cayce about the dream, he confirmed that she needed to see an osteopath, that Lucille was very much aware of what was going on in Rose's and Edward's life together, and that her mother was still trying to help her have a successful pregnancy. The reading called Lucille a "guiding" force and again suggested that Rose needed to prepare herself (physically, mentally, and spiritually) to become pregnant. Rose also mentioned an experience she had encountered one morning when her mother had come to her and claimed, "I am alive," which had startled her awake. Asleep on the couch, Cayce told her: "She *is* alive!" (136–45), again confirming that Lucille was alive in the spirit world, remaining very concerned about her daughter's health and well-being.

Rose found herself pregnant, once again, in the summer of 1926. During the pregnancy, Lucille continued in her role as a "spirit guide," communicating with her daughter on multiple occasions. For example, in November Rose had a dream in which her mother came to her and told her to warn Helen (Lucille's sister; Rose's aunt) that she needed to take precautions against the possibility of an accident. In the dream, Lucille confessed that she would become "sick" if anything happened to Helen. During a reading, Cayce confirmed that Helen was, in fact, in danger of becoming involved in an automobile accident. The warning from Lucille was real. Part of the communication between Cayce and Rose follows:

(Q) One recent morning. Saw my mother. She told me that I should warn my Aunt Helen against an accident. Helen seemed to get into an accident, get badly hurt, and my mother took sick from it.
(A) This, as is presented, is an accident regarding getting injured in an automobile and street car accident. Be warned, then, and warn the body [Helen] as regarding same, see? And when the body keeps in that way of being warned, or keeps from the car, then this may not be expected to happen, for here we have,

as it were, the direct communication of the entity in the spirit plane [Lucille] with the entity in the material plane [Rose] ...This also shows the entity how that the entity in the spirit plane, or spirit entity, is mindful of conditions which transpire, exist, in the material plane, see?

(Q) When is this accident in danger of happening to my Aunt Helen?

(A) Within the present moon's phase . . . Before the waning of the moon, see?

(Q) In what manner?

(A) As given, street car and automobile accident.

(Q) How may it be avoided?

(A) As given. Be warned of riding in either through these phases—that is, until the waning of the moon.　　　136-48

After the reading, Rose told Cayce's office staff that one morning upon awakening, she had been completely startled by a vision of Lucille standing in her bedroom. The same month, Rose had another dream experience in which her mother had warned her that another aunt was on the verge of dying of pneumonia if she did not take the proper precautions. Once again, Cayce confirmed that the information was true and that real communication was taking place between Rose and her mother. (136–50) During that winter, Rose would have additional dreams in which her mother seemed to be a source of encouragement regarding the proper diet, rest, and physical activity she needed to maintain in order to successfully complete her pregnancy.

Rose's husband, Edward, obtained a reading of his own because of an experience that happened during the death of a family friend. While the woman lay dying, she stated aloud that Lucille was in the room and had come to help "guide me over." During Edward's reading, Cayce confirmed that it had been a very real experience and that Lucille had, in fact, helped the woman make the transition to the other side. Perhaps because of that experience as well as because of Rose's ongoing communications with her mother, Edward asked a series of questions about how this kind of interaction with the "spirit plane" was even possible. A portion of that reading follows:

(Q) Is it possible for those that have passed into the spirit plane to at all times communicate with those in the earth plane?

(A) Yes and no—for these conditions are as has been de-scribed—that the necessary way or mode must be prepared; for as this ... Those in the astral plane are not always ready. Those in the physical plane are not always ready ... What conditions arise (is asked) that we in the physical plane

(Q) What physical thing may an individual do to be able to communicate with those that have passed into the spirit plane?

(A) Lay aside the carnal or sensuous mind and desire that those who would use that mentality, that soul, for its vehicle of expression, do so in the manner chosen by that soul; for some communicate in act, in sight, in movement, in voice, in writing, in drawing, in speaking, and in the various forces as are manifest—for force is *one* force ...

(Q) Is the effort for spirit communication as much effort on the part of the spirit entity as the effort that should be made on the part of the material or physical entity?

(A) The force should never be applied, and may never be applied and be real, in either case. The willingness and the desire from both is necessary for the perfect communication, see? Illustrate this same condition by that physical condition as is seen in attunement of either that called radio, or of that called phone, or that of any of that vibratory force as is set by the electron in the material plane. Necessary for the perfect union that each be in accord ...   5756-4

Rose continued to successfully carry the pregnancy while Lucille remained a guardian influence in terms of her and her unborn baby's health. Eventually, Edward described to a group of individuals one of the helpful experiences he and his wife attributed to Lucille's concern and intervention that occurred toward the end of her pregnancy:

... My wife, in the eighth month of pregnancy, developed a severe cold which threatened disastrous effects upon the child she was carrying. After trying many prescriptions and remedies, and each one failing to stop the dangerous cough, she experienced the following vision: Her mother appeared to her and told her that if she would beat the white of an egg and add a little lemon and sugar and take this mixture, her cough would disappear. Upon awakening, she prepared the mixture and took three doses. The cough disappeared, with the final result that a mighty fine baby boy was born.   Background 4863-2

In April 1927, Rose's labor pains started and she was admitted to the hospital in order to give birth to her baby. She was twenty–two years old. She and Edward were very excited that the pregnancy had lasted the entire term. They were excited about finally having their first child. However, very quickly it became apparent that the labor pains were much more intense than either she or doctors had anticipated. Finally, in the midst of her unbearable pain, the doctors administered ether. Edward later wrote a letter to Cayce's office to say that his deceased mother–in–law seemed to be present for the birth. He described Rose as being "doped" and provided the following:

> ... Now, as great an objective demonstration of spirit communication that I have ever seen or hope to witness occurred this afternoon between Rose and her mother, as I was holding her hand ... Hazily she said to me:
>
> "My mother is with me. She has been with me since this morning. See, she is right there!" Then Rose pointed to the other side of the bed from which I was sitting, and indicating a little above her head, again said: "My mother is right there."
>
> "What is she saying to you?" I asked.
>
> "She is telling me of her intense pain in her eye and head while she was sick and telling me to be brave in my pain now. She is bearing me up—I never could keep up my courage, but for her being with me. She is right here with me - has been all day."
>
> "What is she saying?" I asked [again] ...
>
> "She is saying," replied Rose clearly and precisely, "not to worry—that everything is coming out alright!"

"How do you know she is here with you?" I asked.

"I feel her—I see her—she is praying for me—she is here right with me—right there," and again Rose pointed her hand to the same exact location.

Now I ask you, have you ever heard of anything so wonderful?

Poor little kid [Rose] ... longing for her mother on this day of suffering more than ever, feels and knows that her loved one is with her and hears from her ... I tell you, when I came out and told five grown folks about this, including my very practical mother, every one of them cried like babies. Darn it, I am bawling as I write it. It sort of has me in a daze—I don't know just how to be grateful enough or what to do. It's so wonderful, so definite, so precise, so beautiful that it is far beyond me.

Background 136-59

Rose gave birth to a son. Although doctors remained concerned about her physical health, both baby and mother were fine. Unfortunately, Edward reported to the Cayce office that the same day his wife gave birth, Rose's father had committed suicide at his home in Louisiana. Although the older man had been sick, no one had expected him to commit suicide, and the fact that it had occurred on the same day as the baby's birth was horribly tragic. Because his wife was still weak, he and the doctors thought it best not to tell Rose of her father's death until later. In a letter to Edgar Cayce, Edward made note the following:

... Everyone up here is just horror struck, and sometimes as she [Rose] talks of taking her baby to see its granddad in ..., La., we have got to fight hard to keep back the tears from coming right in front of her. He wrote her a letter just before, on April 6th, congratulating her ... It is going to be a terrible shock when it comes and of course not telling her is only postponing it ...

Report 136-59

During that week, Rose told her husband that she had dreamt the following: "My sister phoned me from New Orleans to tell me that my father was desperately sick and the doctors gave little hope." (136–60) The dream became part of the impetus encouraging Edward to tell her what happened. Later that fall, Rose had another dream in which both her mother and father came to warn her that Rose's sister, Patricia, was contemplating suicide due to her own depression. During the reading, Cayce advised Rose that her parents were depending on her to help her sister through this time of crisis. (136–70) Prior to Thanksgiving that year, Rose had another dream in which she was giving Milk of Magnesia to her son. Cayce told her that the guidance had come from her mother because the child was having issues with his stomach being too acidic. She was advised to administer Milk of Magnesia. (136–75) Several months later, Lucille came to Rose again in a dream as reassurance that she remained very much aware of her daughter's activities. In the dream, Rose asked her mother if she had been able to speak to her father? Lucille stated that she had seen and apparently spoken to him but that they were on "different planes" of existence. (136–78) Ongoing communication between Rose and her mother continued. Rose's subconscious mind had a heightened ability to tune into her mother, especially in the dream state.

Finally in March 1930, Rose had her last reading from Edgar Cayce. She was thinking of about having another pregnancy before year's end. She was still receiving guidance from her deceased mother and wondered how such communication was able to be maintained. She also asked during the reading whether or not it was possible for an individual to consciously keep in touch with and specifically choose a guide who remained in the spirit plane. Cayce replied that it was possible but that it could also be problematic and he called to mind the story in 1 Samuel 28 in which the deceased prophet, Samuel, was disturbed by Saul, the first King of Israel, causing Samuel to ask: "Why disturbest thou me?" (136–83) The insinuation was not to specifically seek out a guide but to instead use the information if it was sent, helpful, and relevant.

Unfortunately for Rose and Edward, later that year Edward became infatuated with another woman. He and Rose divorced. She did not remarry nor did she ever have another child. For a time, she relocated to Louisiana to be near her sister. It would be more than twenty years before she would contact Cayce's office again—nearly ten years after

Edgar Cayce's passing—and confirm how helpful the Cayce information had been to her during those four years. There is no further indication in her file as to whether or not her mother continued in the role of spirit guide.

Although offering far fewer stories and much less documentation, a similar example of a deceased parent acting in the role of a spirit guide is evidenced in the case of a thirty–seven–year–old dentist who frequently dreamed about his father. In 1942, he obtained a life reading in which he was told that he had been among the Israelites who had journeyed out of Egypt and had wandered in the wilderness for forty years. In spite of hardship, however, during that period he had been able to hold fast to both his faith and the law of his faith. During that reading the dentist inquired, "Please advise me regarding my association with my father, [...] (deceased), who often appears to me in dreams. Is he my spiritual guide?" Cayce responded that his father had acted in the capacity of "guide and guard" during that period in the wilderness and was attempting to do so again. That said, the ultimate influence that his father was hoping to bring to him was the awareness of spiritual guidance found in his own faith. (2772-1)

Previously, the dentist's wife had reported that although she had never met her father–in–law and knew him only through family pictures, as he had died before their marriage, he had appeared to her during her difficult labor. At the time, she did not know the sex of the child (a boy). She told her husband that she had seen a distinct vision of his father: "He took my head in his hands, turned it back away from him, to look at you." She turned and saw that her husband was standing with a son in his arms. She told her husband, "Your father sent me to you with a baby boy." (Report 2779-1)

The role of deceased relatives as spirit guides was revisited while discussing the karmic connections between Edgar Cayce, his wife, Gertrude, and his secretary, Gladys Davis. As background information, the readings suggest that patterns from the past frequently draw individuals back together as a means of enabling them to "meet" themselves and ultimately experience soul growth in the process. Because of this dynamic, a cyclic pattern of reincarnation can be viewed in the lives of a number of Cayce's contemporaries. One example is that a number of people who had readings were given a series of lifetimes that often included the following: Atlantis, ancient Egypt, Palestine, Europe, Colonial America, and then as a contemporary of Edgar Cayce's in the twentieth century.[16]

It was because of this oft-repeated pattern and the fact that neither Gertrude nor Gladys received past-life information about a Palestinian incarnation that both of them asked about it in subsequent readings. In the case of Gladys, she inquired, "Have I had a Palestine incarnation?" and the response came: "Very close to the activities of same, but within those realms of the spiritual rather than in the material manifestations; though close, and an impelling influence in the affairs and experiences of many . . . " (288-45)

In her own reading, Gertrude asked, "Have I had a Palestine incarnation? and what am I meeting in the present from same?" Cayce replied, "We do not find such as an influence in the present; being more of a vision of than an experience in that environment . . . these were rather close in the union of purpose and activities through experiences other than in the earth's sojourn." Her follow-up question was, "What has caused the feeling of having had an experience at some time in Palestine?" And the response: "The influences or forces that overshadowed the activities through those experiences; because of the union of purpose in these two individuals just named [Gertrude and Gladys] in their activity or vision over, or influencing of those activities of individuals, see?" In other words, Gertrude and Gladys had been in the spirit realm during that period assisting Edgar Cayce as spirit guides when he had been an individual named Lucius. Lucius had been a follower of Jesus and involved with the Church of Laodicea (one of the seven churches mentioned in Revelation). Gertrude's reading went on to suggest that both she and Gladys had been very much involved as "guardian angels" for Edgar Cayce in that lifetime:

> . . . For they became then what might be termed as guardian angels. See, these are the conditions—study this, that you may perfectly understand: The sojourn of a soul-entity other than in materiality often influences or bears weight with individuals

---

[16]Kevin J. Todeschi, *Edgar Cayce on the Akashic Records* (Virginia Beach, VA: A.R.E. Press, 1998), 15.

within the material plane—as an odor, a scent, an emotion, a wave, a wind upon the activities. Such are termed or called by some guardian angels, or influences that would promote activities for weal or for woe. *Thus* does the association of individuals at times become as an influence in the activities of individuals through particular periods or experiences. Thus, when there is a description of that period, or an emotion that arises from such influences, or a knowledge of conditions at such a period, there is then the wave of emotion that would seem to connect or associate with that period ...   538-59

A forty-six-year-old business executive and member of the American Society for Psychical Research obtained several readings dealing with his health, business advice, and the topic of reincarnation. Interested in spiritualism, the individual claimed that he had a connection with a spirit guide named Azuab. During one of his readings, he wanted to confirm if he really had spirit guides; the reading responded:

Each and every soul has its guides that may be designated by the desires of the inmost self. In the realm of spirit many may seek to give that which may be of interest, and at times of aid, to individuals seeking from such realms; yet—as the promise has been unto the sons of men—He, the Lord, *is* sufficient unto thee. Then, that which may be the greater, the better guide to each and every soul, is that of self through its associations—its own associations—in the spirit realm ... Hence seek in self the more, and that which is answered first in self on any subject. Where material or mental aid is sought, *answer* the problem in the consciousness of self. *Then* seek a verification in the period of meditation. And *this* aid will be the greater.   423-2

During a subsequent reading, he asked Cayce to "Please give name and history of highest spirit guide assigned to my wife and me?" The response came:

These had best be sought in self. Not that these may not be given, for they are present with thee in thy activities; but "What is thy name?" that has been sought by others, and as the answer came then, "What meanest these experiences in thy life?" so may the name come to thee, even as it did to Elkanah [Elkanah—1 Sam. 1:21; husband of Hannah, father of Samuel] as he offered the sacrifice, as he offered meat—for he is thy guide.

Looking for more clarification, the businessman asked, "Has he any instructions as for our contact with him?" Cayce responded:

Seek and ye shall find. Put into application that thou knowest day by day, for it is line upon line, precept upon precept, here a little and there a little that ye gather together those forces that make for the greater material manifestation of those influences in thy daily experience that may bring thee to the conscious-ness, to the understanding of those forces that would aid thee. For, as has been given, when thou hast shown in thine heart thy willingness to be guided and directed by *His* force, He gives His angels charge concerning thee that they bear thee up and prevent the stumblings that come to the sons of the Creative Forces in and among the sons of men. Hence keep—keep—true to self and to that thou knowest, for the way is open before thee. Seek rather to show thyself as one worthy of acceptance to the God influence that is shown in man's experience through the manifestations of His Son in the earth; for He is thy guide, *He* will show thee the way. His brethren, His brothers in the activities in the earth, may show thee thy way.

Finally the question was asked, "Who is A-z-u-a-b?"

One that would make known much, but seek—seek—seek; yet thou knowest, as in thine earthly experience, knowledge without the use of that thou knowest comes to naught. He will be near, but let him make manifest—let him speak the *name;* for *he, he,* will guide when thou hast prepared thine self for the greater work that lies just ahead. Give glory, then, to the Father through His Son, that He hast thought, He hast shown, He hast manifest in His relationships with thee that thou art worthy of

> acceptation for a definite activity in thine experience ... For, as thou walkest in the way that brings life, light and hope into the experience of thy brother, so may His joy—that passeth understanding—be in thine heart and quicken thy soul as to being near with Him.
>
> 423-3

On another occasion, a thirty–five–year–old woman wrote Edgar Cayce to ask for his assistance. She had served in her father's lumber and manufacturing business as both bookkeeper and secretary. Her father had died suddenly, and thus she and her sister were confused as to what to do with the family business. Her letter asked, "Is it best for my sister and me to sell our interests or to remain in the business . . . ?" The reading suggested that her father remained very much concerned about the business and was ready to serve in the capacity of guide, providing her with assistance in managing the business. She would get that assistance in the form of intuitive information that came to her. The reading went on to state that although her father had frequently given thought to selling the business on his own, it always remained a part of him. The reading suggested she would have the very same feelings:

> ... While there were periods when the father expressed the desire to be rid of, or to have a change in the business relations, yet the business of the company was such that it remained, and remains, near to the inmost being of the body. So the same conditions exist in the mind and inmost elements of this body ...
>
> 4651-1

Cayce added that there were other executives within the company who were very much committed to its success, but their judgment was not always as good as her father's. Her younger brother also had potential as a company executive, but the fruition of that would be several years away. She needed to decide what she wanted to do. If she decided to keep the company, her father would remain as a guide helping her with the decisions. If she decided to sell the company, her father would turn loose of his influence upon the business. Cayce's final piece of advice was: "These decisions *must be made in self!*"

A woman who was part of her Methodist church's prayer group

obtained a reading because she continuously felt the presence of her deceased brother. This experience often occurred at night when she would awaken suddenly and literally feel his presence in her room. She asked Cayce for an explanation of what was occurring; he replied, "This is a reality." On another occasion she had heard his voice calling her. Again, Cayce stated that this was a reality and had occurred when her brother, "found the attunement such as to speak with thee." Rather than he being a guide for her, however, the reading suggested that she could serve in the role as a guide for him. Apparently, he needed her prayers to completely make the transition. When the woman inquired if there was anything that her brother wanted her to know, the reading explained:

> Much that he needs of thee. Forget not to pray for and with him; not seeking to hold him but that he, too, may walk the way to the light, in and through the experience. For this is well. Those who have passed on need the prayers of those who live aright. For the prayers of those who would be righteous in spirit may save many who have erred, even in the flesh.   3416-1

Another woman wrote to say that she truly missed her deceased mother, "So often I can just feel what Mother would say to me, were she here. I will never cease to miss her every minute of my life." The two women had apparently been like sisters, as her mother's nickname for her was "Sister." She had a dream in which her mother came to her and told her that she loved her. When the woman obtained a reading to see how this was possible, Cayce began by stating: "The dreams, as we see, come to individuals through the subjugation of the conscious mind, and the subconscious being of the soul—when loosed—is able to communicate with the subconscious minds of those whether in the material or the cosmic plane." Shortly thereafter, there was an interruption and the woman's mother seemed to be present, speaking through Edgar Cayce (although using his voice):

> Sister—Sister—as is seen by you, Mother sees, Mother knows, Mother feels those same feelings of that love which is in the earth that makes of the heavenly home. And while I am in the

> spirit planes I am yet present in the minds and hearts of those who express to me the love as builded in the being—the love the Master shows to all ... for Mother does not leave you, Sister—and Mother knows! 243-5

The woman was convinced that her mother remained a guide, guard, and a "living angel" in her life.

A forty–year–old single woman worked both as a writer and part–time as a secretary for her employer, with whom she had fallen in love. He was a prominent doctor, speaker, and writer, and had separated from his first wife. The doctor had lost two of his adult children (a son and a daughter) to death. In addition to being in love with the doctor, the woman was also somehow psychically connected to the deceased children (especially the son) and occasionally felt them as a presence in her life. In fact, on one occasion the woman noted that one of the children had apparently tried to send her a message by tapping on the bathroom mirror while she was brushing her teeth. (1210-5). Because the doctor had not divorced his wife, the woman felt guilt about their ongoing relationship and wondered whether or not she should leave her position. At the same time, she could not turn loose of her intense attraction to him. Part of her reading was focused on what she should do about the situation:

> (Q) Is this situation a karmic condition brought about by me in the past and if so under what circumstances? How can I straighten it out now?
>
> (A) Ye are constantly meeting thyself—but do not think because they are thy problems that no one else has ever had same ... There are *thousands* upon *thousands* that are ever, and are to-day, meeting themselves just as thyself! Karma may be lost in Him, if ye will but seek, if ye will but have Him guide, if ye will but believe! For all power hath been given unto Him. For He *alone* hath overcome! And doth He forgive, doth He stand by? Only when ye individually or personally put Him from thee, and turn *thy face* away, is He from thee at all! For His great promise has been in these: "Be my child—I will be thy God. Though ye wander far afield, though ye may be discouraged, disheartened,

> if ye call I will *hear*—and will answer speedily." O Child, put Him
> in thy heart and try Him!   954-5

The woman asked whether or not the deceased son's influence was helpful on herself and her employer. Cayce's reply suggested that the ongoing communication was not intended to guide her in one direction or another but to instead provide reassurance of the continuity of life. When the woman wanted to know what kind of an effect the influence was having upon her thinking, the reply came:

> Only to that extent as ye allow him to have an effect! Who is thy God? Who is thy Way? In Whom do ye live and move? Is not the Father in Jesus Christ the Lord of all? Is He not God of the living, whether they be in spirit, in mind or in body? Then why *question* ye? These communications come as *assurances,* not as guides, not as directors! For He *alone* is the Way! He *alone* is the Truth! Then *why*—*why* harken to that which will *only* bring confusion, when ye confuse thy ideal?

In addition to angels and spirit guides, the Edgar Cayce readings occasionally discussed another spiritual being called an "elemental." Edgar Cayce's personal interest in elementals really started when he had been a child. Born in the Kentucky countryside, he often played with fairies, pixies, brownies, and other creatures that no other children could see—except for his little friend, Anna. For several years, Anna was his closest and most consistent companion. Unfortunately she passed away from pneumonia when she was only twelve years old in 1888. Imagine Edgar Cayce's surprise more than fifty years later when, in 1940, he gave a reading to a twenty-nine-year-old woman and told her that before her present lifetime she had been Anna! From that point forward until Edgar Cayce's own death, the woman, her husband, and Edgar Cayce became close friends and often communicated via letter. In Cayce's correspondence he described some of the childhood experiences they had encountered with the "little folk" of the forest. Excerpts from a couple of his letters follow:

> Yes—we used it when we used to play together, do not know

that it was the little folk who told us, or was just chance—but we used it first to play house for we always played we were keeping house together—we were the little home builders right ... We played in the Church yard and the wood around same, and there were more pretty Violets in that wood—they must still be your favorite flower—for they were then and many the day you had your little arms full of them ...

We had played often with the little folks in the barn stable and the strawrick near the stables, but had not known the Fairies or the prixies [pixies] of the water or creek. Do not recall that we had read any thing in particular about these folks before that day. We had taken the little folks as being a very natural occurrence and as have said all through you and I rather curious to believe in such things except my mother and Mr. B. A. each of them thought we were very unusual but a very pretty idea at least—and after the day told you of in the Barn when Mr. B. A. played for us and we told him of the days with the little folk was much easier for you and I—anyway this day—as I recall it must have been about the time of day we should have been going to S.S. [Sunday school] or church but we went exploring and went to the Creek, met John near the spring. He told us again of the Island and lent us his boat to go there. We went—and found it a very lovely beautiful spot—the little folks came almost immediately we landed—soon we builded us a lovely little play house with the help of the little folks. There were then several of them, say some four or five boys and girls like our selves—among the flowers we saw the Fairies for the first time—learned from the little folks the difference between the Fairies and prixies [pixies] and the Gnomes. There we pledged ourselves to one another for all time, witnessed by the little folks and blessed by the Fairies— sang to by the prixies [pixies], and guess we might have stayed on and on but late in the evening we were called home by your Mother and Josie your older sister. Oh yes we went again to the island, and yet again until it was too cold to go—even tho we both got whippings for going, but it was beautiful there—a real fairy land.   Reports 2072-6 and 2072-10

In addition to Edgar Cayce's personal experiences, on occasion other individuals received readings that confirmed the existence of these creatures—various forms of life in the spirit plane that can have an influence upon humankind. Oftentimes, the case histories in the Cayce files suggest that children especially are prone to seeing these "little folk," perhaps because they are much more open psychically or perhaps because the activities of the material world have yet to squelch their sensitivity to such things. For example, a forty–nine–year–old engineer wrote that he was especially sensitive to the spiritual side of life as a youth and often saw "peculiar visions of brownies, elves, etc., in a very pronounced manner" between the ages of four and fourteen. (Report 333-1)

In 1938, while giving a life reading to the aunt of a baby girl who was only eighteen–days–old, Cayce encouraged the parents to help the child develop her "imaginative forces." He also suggested that the child would benefit from experiences in nature and would be positively influenced by the "little folk" that would be a part of those experiences:

> Things then that have to do with the outdoors, with forest, with streams, with those things having to do especially with horticultural nature, will be of special interest to the entity.
> And the little folk that inhabit many a dell will be a guiding force for the entity, if there is care taken *when* it is in active influence during its early periods of development out of doors. Plenty of sunshine, then, should ever be the experience for the entity. Not as one wild, no—but as one well-regulated, with a great deal of close communion with nature.   1775-1

The positive influence of these creatures was also cited in a reading given for a fourteen–year–old girl who had talent as an artist. Her reading encouraged her to pursue both music and art, " . . . especially in that field of art which would be designated as place cards, Christmas pictures, [and] season's greetings . . . " Parents were told that the girl was especially psychic and that those abilities were to be encouraged, not submerged. Cayce said that she had a lifetime in Persia in which she had been attracted to Grecian culture and art and had also developed a keen interest in the mystical and—what the reading called—"nature's dwellers." That interest would manifest in the present with an ability to see these same creatures. Part of the girl's reading included the following:

> ...Do apply self in the direction especially of art and music. For these will offer the channels, especially as has been indicated, through which not only the material success may be gained but the interpretation of the physical, the spiritual, the psychic. Don't be afraid to acknowledge that ye see fairies as ye study, for you will nurture these experiences. Don't be afraid to say that you see the gnomes which would hinder peoples at times. These may be a part of the background for many of the cards, for many of the various sketches which you would make.
>
> 5359-1

On another occasion, parents of a four-year-old boy were told that their child was especially attuned to things of spiritual nature and that he was extremely psychic. This combination would apparently give the child insights and ideas, causing the parents to sometimes wonder where their son was obtaining his information. For that reason, they were advised, "*Do not question* the entity as to the sources of his information. *Do not correct* the entity as to that given, but keep a detailed record of what is given." The reading traced the boy's psychic sensitivity to a past life in Scotland when he had been very much attuned to the creatures of nature. It was apparently an attunement that the child brought with him into the present:

> Before this the entity was in the Scotch land. The entity began its activity as a prodigy, as one already versed in its associations with the unseen—or the elemental forces; the fairies and those of every form that do not give expression in a material way and are only seen by those who are attuned to the infinite. 2547-1

The influence of these creatures in the lives of adults was also cited by the readings on numerous occasions. For example, a thirty-nine-year-old sales manager was trying to decide the proper approach to pursuing a business deal with another individual. His reading suggested that the best approach was simply to follow-through on his personal judgment regarding the project. Cayce stated that he could also talk about the project with others and get their comparative advice, or he could just wait and ponder the situation until " . . . the little brownies come along and tell him what to do! . . . " (257–87)

A similar discussion occurred in a reading given to a wildcat oil driller who asked whether or not he could get guidance on drilling wells from a psychic source. Cayce's response was that it was best to get the guidance from within rather than from without. That guidance would present itself in the form of intuition, and it would be intuition coming from brownies that surrounded the individual. Perhaps not fully understanding what the term meant, the oil driller asked: "What is meant by the term "brownies" in the last answer . . . " Cayce replied:

> The manner in which those of the elementals—entities who have not entered into materiality—have manifested and do at times manifest themselves before or to the entity, [1265]. Brownies, pixies, fairies, gnomes are not elementals, but elements that are as definite *entities* as man materialized, see?
>
> 1265-3

Conversely, a woman who was having problems with her addict husband and under a great deal of mental strain, was told that her stress and her nervousness had caused her to become sensitive to the influence of others, and she was warned to protect herself from coming under the influence of things outside of herself: "Beware of outer influences, or coming under the control of individuals or elementals." (4340–1)

In 1932, Edgar Cayce gave a reading on the topic of " . . . communication with entities in the spirit or fourth dimensional plane and the laws that govern such communication . . . " The reading began by suggesting that throughout history individuals who had been open to the influence of guides and spirits had often been labeled and judged as being wizards and witches. Questions were asked about the nature of spirit communication, including the following:

> (Q) Does the communication between those who have passed into the spirit plane and those on the earth depend on previously established relationships, on understanding and love, or upon what?

(A) "As the tree falleth so will it lie." Because there are changes in the dimensional conditions does not alter that which is known in the earth plane as desire. If the desire is in that direction that there may be an association with, an aid to, a seeking of such associations, then only the means, the channel, the way, the course, is necessary to complete the communication. The attunement of that materially known as the radio may offer an illustration for this. If there is the desire that the communication be with those from plane to plane, the attunement of an individual in the material or earth plane to the attunement of the entity in the spirit or fourth dimensional plane is necessary ...

(Q) Does communication further or retard, or not affect, the spiritual progression of those in spirit life?

(A) It does all! There are the same elements as in material; for, as *is* known, that which has materialized into matter is of the elements that are dematerializing, or dematerialized, and where aid may be lent there must be the desire. Even as seen, known, understood by many, those desires have carried an entity on to heights that are detrimental to be called into association with purely materialization, or material, for all are given to that to which they have attuned or builded, that that is of both the material and spiritual essence of truth, fact, condition, whether positive, negative, or static.   5756-8

A sixty–five–year–old woman who was extremely psychic and open to the influence of entities in the spirit plane wanted to know how she could determine whether or not the influence was a positive one. She inquired, "How can I discern the helpful entities or forces from those forces that would do me harm?" Cayce's response was as follows:

In each experience ask that they acknowledge the life, the death, the resurrection of the Jesus, the Christ. They that answer only as in the affirmative; otherwise, "Get thee behind me I will have no part with thee. Through His name only *will* I, [422], *accept* direction!"   422-1

The centrality of the role of Jesus in assisting all of humankind was also brought to mind in a reading given to an ecumenical spiritual growth group. During the course of the reading one of the individuals asked about a vision she had seen. Cayce's response encouraged her to place her focus in the proper direction—it was the same response he would give on multiple occasions to individuals interested in seeking information from guides and discarnates in the spirit realm:

> ... Pray rather to the Son, the Father through the Son, that He walks with thee—and He *will* walk and talk with thee. Be *not* satisfied with *any* other. He may oft give His angels charge concerning thee, yet know the Master's touch, the Master's voice; for He may walk and talk with thee. *He* is the Way; there is no other. He in body suffered; for himself, yea—for thee also. Wilt thou turn, then, to any other? 5749-4

3

The Angels Speak:
Michael, the Lord of the Way

When Edgar Cayce gave a reading, he would lie down on a couch, close his eyes, begin to pray, and wait for the suggestion that would prompt his unconscious mind to tune into the subject that he was being asked to explore in the psychic state. The suggestion he received for a Life Reading—one dealing with exploring an individual's past lives and how that person had "gained" or "lost" from the perspective of soul growth—was as follows:

> You will give the relation of this entity and the Universe, and the Universal Forces, giving the conditions that are as personalities latent and exhibited in the present life. Also the former appearances in the earth's plane, giving time, place and the name, and that in that life which built or retarded the development for the entity, giving the abilities of the present entity and to that which it may attain, and how.   953-13

When the topic being explored was related to the physical health of the individual, the suggestion was more like the following:

> You will have before you the body and enquiring mind of [2398], present in this room, who seeks information, advice and guidance, as to his health, his mental and material affairs and associations. You will go over his body carefully, examine it thoroughly, and tell me the conditions you find at the present time; giving cause of the existing conditions, also suggestions for correction ...Then you will answer the questions, as I ask them, concerning his mental and material welfare.   2398-1

In addition to the above, there were suggestions related to a myriad of topics, such as for the "Work readings" that helped Cayce's unconscious mind tune into aspects of the Cayce work and its future. There were suggestions for business advice, dream interpretation, and various types of symbolism, mental–spiritual counsel, the study group material (focusing on personal soul growth), etc. Regardless of the suggestion, however, according to those who witnessed dozens or even hundreds of readings, when Edgar Cayce spoke in the unconscious state, it was with his normal voice and cadence. However, in July 1928, at the end of a reading that was given to explore the Work of the Association of National Investigators (the precursor to Edgar Cayce's A.R.E.), the association that built the Cayce Hospital, someone else with an extremely powerful voice seemed to speak through Edgar Cayce.

Cayce has just finished explaining how the Work was essentially to become an "educational factor" for anyone who became involved with the association. He also discussed that the board of the organization should work with one another in "wholehearted cooperation." He even went on to discuss various roles and efforts that would be required of specific board members. He finished by describing what should be engraved on the cornerstone of the Cayce Hospital building: "That we may make manifest the love of God and man," and then to everyone's surprise the intensity and volume of Cayce's voice changed as it announced that it was the archangel Michael who was now coming through. In order to capture the formidable nature of the commanding presence those in the room heard, Cayce's secretary, Gladys Davis, took most of the words down in capital letters:

> HARK! There comes the voice of one who would speak to those gathered here: (Pause) I AM MICHAEL, LORD OF THE WAY! BEND THY HEAD, OH YE CHILDREN OF MEN! GIVE HEED UNTO THE WAY AS IS SET BEFORE YOU IN THAT SERMON ON THE MOUNT, IN THAT ON YON HILL THIS ENLIGHTENMENT MAY COME AMONG MEN; FOR EVEN AS THE VOICE OF THE ONE WHO STOOD BESIDE THE SEA AND CALLED ALL MEN UNTO THE WAY, THAT THOSE THAT WOULD HARKEN MIGHT KNOW THERE WAS AGAIN A STAFF IN DAVID, AND THE ROD OF JESSE HAS NOT FAILED: FOR IN ZION THY NAMES ARE WRITTEN, AND IN SERVICE WILL COME TRUTH! 254-42

Although it was the first time that the powerful voice would make an appearance during the course of a reading, it would not be the last. Over the next sixteen years, Michael would come through without warning on more than a dozen occasions.

Within days of the archangel's appearance, Edgar Cayce would communicate with several of the largest supporters of his work, including Morton Blumenthal, David Kahn, and Tim Brown, calling it "one of the most interesting readings on the work we have ever had." Because the angelic voice had referred to the Sermon on the Mount (Matt. 5–7), known for such things as "Blessed are the pure in heart," and "Ye are the light of the world," and "seek first the kingdom of God," and admonitions to hold fast to faith and to not worry about tomorrow, Cayce was convinced that the message was about the importance of those being connected with the work seeking mercy, grace, and "at–onement" with Him.

More than anyone else at the time, Morton Blumenthal was Edgar Cayce's principal financial backer. Early on, Morton had excelled as a stockbroker, providing the wherewithal to move the Cayce family to Virginia Beach. In addition to supporting the Cayce family, he underwrote the construction of the Cayce hospital and the founding of Atlantic University, the first university in Virginia Beach. Only in his thirties, he was also extremely intelligent, gifted as a writer and speaker, and although Jewish, was convinced that the Cayce information on

Jesus as "an Elder brother" who showed each soul the way back to at-onement with the Creator was reconcilable with every individual's faith. Because Morton's backing and passion were instrumental during the early years and the archangel Michael appeared to be supportive of the Cayce endeavor, it was not surprising that the archangel would next make his presence known in three of Morton's readings the following year.

In January 1929, during a reading focusing on business advice, Morton's younger brother, Edwin, asked about the difference between some of the business hunches he often had and the phenomenon of "visions." Cayce's reply was that essentially both operated from the same principle, although one was a higher level associated with spiritual development. When Edwin asked about the vibration associated with these experiences, Cayce replied that ultimately all vibration was associated with the Creator and the destiny of humankind was to essentially make its vibration at-one with God. After Edwin asked for additional information about a past-life when he had been among the tribes of Israel and Cayce responded, the archangel Michael came through:

> . . . Hark! There would come Him the Lord of the Way [Michael, the archangel], and he would speak with thee: "Bow thine head, for unto *thee* is committed *now* the keeping of that way in the earth that [man] may know that the rod has not departed from Judah, neither has the lion been allayed that rose up in Midian, and unto Him that thou would counsel in teaching my people the ways. Lord of Hosts, be thou near as this, thy servant, bows and calls on those forces as were manifest in the flesh in the way as goeth down by Bethsaida, and as were gathered in the house of Joseph—as in Capernaum many came and kneeled and called thy servant blessed. *He* now is given that charge of he that goes as the light to his people."
> We are through.   900-422

In addition to referencing the rod or staff of Judah (Gen. 49:10), which is associated with the lineage of the soul who would become the Christ, and the early days of the ministry of Jesus, the information seemed to suggest that the Blumenthals were being instrumental in helping the "light" (perhaps in the form of the Cayce information) go out to humankind.

Two months later, Morton Blumenthal obtained another reading in which he sought information on how the Cayce work could help not only individuals who were beginners in terms of spiritual principles but also those who were more advanced. The reading's advice was that it was well to seek information that would be applicable to individuals, but it was also important to remember that the dissemination of that information would not necessarily make Morton's own life easier or without challenge. In spite of these challenges, however, he was assured that he would be guided by those in the spiritual realm, including the archangel Michael. He was also told to remain steadfast in his resolve and given the following personal advice:

> ...Be not led then astray in any manner, not allowing self to be drawn from these ways as may be pointed out, and even as has been given there will come the ability—in the application of the knowledge gained—the understanding as is being sought. Be not dictatorial, nor lording in thine own activity. Rather humble in spirit ...as the knowledge comes let *it* be disseminated among those who seek ...Through thine efforts then, my son, be faithful ...   900-428

In May of that year, Morton was getting a reading dealing with practical business advice, including how Cayce might revise a pamphlet for those who were seeking help. Archangel Michael again came through in an exchange that suggested the importance of attracting and then helping seekers "scattered far afield." The Cayce work was being encouraged to somehow find a way to seek out those who wanted help in discovering their own path back to God:

> (Q) Regarding the second edition of the pamphlet ...is it in good shape?
> (A) It's in good shape to be *gotten* in good shape! to be delivered to those who are seeking—much better, far better understanding will be gained. Gradually work in more now of that of individual experience, also that of *some* elements of the

spectacular—but keep the reason! for ever should it *ever* be, "Come let us reason together." Never my way, but thine, O lord, be done! for him who would guide, guard and direct the efforts of these bodies [Michael, the archangel?] would approach for just a word.

Bow down thine head, my son, and seek the Lord while He may be found. Forsake not the tenets of thy fathers, and forget not the Lord in David gave, "For my servant David's sake will I remember mine people, even though they be scattered far afield," and let us gather unto the gate and behold the glory of the Son, even as He walks in the way—for the Father pitieth His children who love His ways and keeps them, though they wander afield, yet will the hearts be kept singing, in thy house will they be gathered ...   900-442

In a follow-up reading given to explore the possibility of creating a world organization that could help all of humankind establish "hospitals, churches, schools, farm loans, rural road constructions" and so forth "throughout all the nations," the sleeping Cayce suggested that such an undertaking would require all of those involved to be steadfast in living their spiritual ideals. He went on to suggest that it could only be accomplished one step at a time ("line upon line") as each lived up to that which they said they believed, and that each individual needed to eradicate from self those things that were not of the spirit. At that point, Michael spoke:

Hark! Ye children of men bow thine head, for Michael the Lord of the Way would show *thee* thine way—Who is able to stand in the day of the Lord? He that has purified his heart in the ways that make for the sons of men to know the Lord of Hosts *would* approach to thine own throne; for *who* is this Lord? He that is *holy* is His name! Amen.   3976-7

In August 1931, a message from the archangel presented itself during a reading given to a prominent bandleader and conductor who was interested in spirit communication. In an effort to apparently verify the accuracy of the Cayce information, the individual asked about an angelic entity named "Azul," whom he had either picked up on intuitively or had heard about from another psychic. When he asked the sleeping Cayce if he could contact Azul for him, the response was a definitive "No." Cayce suggested that an individual's "sincerity in purpose" had a vibrational impact upon the source and quality of the readings. In other words, to obtain such information simply to prove the accuracy of that being given was an improper intent. The bandleader rephrased his query, as follows: "Can you contact Azul for anyone else?" It was then that Michael spoke, suggesting that the ultimate source was neither angels nor spirit guides but the Christ Himself:

> Not under these conditions; for I, Michael, speak as the Lord of the Way. Bow thine heads, O ye peoples, that would seek to know the mysteries of that life as makes for those *faltering* steps in men's lives when not applied in the manner as has been laid down. O ye stiff-necked and adulterous generation! Who *will* approach the Throne that ye may know that there is *none* that surpasses the Son of Man in His approach to *human* experience in the material world!   2897-4

While a few readings explored the possibility of a larger organization to assist all of humankind, nothing ever manifested. Instead, the focus of the work remained with the Blumenthals, the hospital, and Atlantic University. Unfortunately, within a few years there would be a break between the Blumenthal brothers and Edgar Cayce. Part of the challenge stemmed from the fact that although other wealthy individuals were a part of the Work, the Blumenthals were the only ones that were consistent in funding. Because of this tremendous financial commitment, Morton Blumenthal felt that his needs in terms of the readings should take precedence over everybody else; Cayce felt otherwise. Edgar Cayce was also not a good financial manager, obviously causing stress for the Blumenthals who were underwriting both the hospital and the university. To make matters worse, there was jealousy between Morton and Cayce's longtime friend, David Kahn. In time, the Blumenthals withdrew their financial backing, and both the Cayce hospital and Atlantic University were closed.

While all of this was occurring, a group of Cayce's supporters gathered together to understand how they might best continue to work with Edgar Cayce's psychic information. Beginning in September 1931, the group came together for readings that could not only be helpful for them but would encourage Cayce to continue his work in spite of losing the hospital. What may have begun as a simple series of meetings soon turned to a dedicated focus on the nature of spiritual growth and personal transformation. The group worked to compile spiritual growth lessons that could be applicable to all individuals. Beginning with a lesson entitled "Cooperation," what followed was a series of twenty-three additional lessons over the next decade. The group's intent was that these lessons could be applied, understood, even "lived" so that a true awareness of the living Spirit would become possible in daily life. Eventually, the group procured 130 readings on the topic and publish the lessons as *A Search for God* information.

During 1932, the archangel Michael came through these study group readings on four different occasions, suggesting that the promise that had originally been given to the work underwritten by the Blumenthals was still intact. In fact, during a reading given in September 1932, Michael interrupted and told the group:

BE STILL, MY CHILDREN! BOW THINE HEADS, THAT THE LORD OF THE WAY MAY MAKE KNOWN UNTO YOU THAT HAVE BEEN CHOSEN FOR A SERVICE IN THIS PERIOD WHEN THERE IS THE NEED OF THAT SPIRIT BEING MADE MANIFEST IN THE EARTH, THAT THE WAY MAY BE KNOWN TO THOSE THAT SEEK THE LIGHT! FOR THE GLORY OF THE FATHER WILL BE MADE MANIFEST THROUGH YOU THAT ARE FAITHFUL UNTO THE CALLING WHEREIN THOU HAST BEEN CALLED! YE THAT HAVE NAMED THE NAME MAKE KNOWN IN THY DAILY WALKS OF LIFE, IN THE LITTLE ACTS OF THE LESSONS THAT HAVE BEEN BUILDED IN THINE OWN EXPERIENCE, THROUGH THOSE ASSOCIATIONS OF SELF IN MEDITATION AND PRAYER, THAT HIS WAY MAY BE KNOWN AMONG MEN: FOR HE CALLS ON ALL—WHOSOEVER WILL MAY COME—AND HE STANDS AT THE DOOR OF THINE OWN CONSCIENCE, THAT YE MAY BE AWARE THAT THE SCEPTER HAS NOT DEPARTED FROM ISRAEL, NOR HAVE HIS WAYS BEEN IN VAIN: FOR TODAY, WILL YE HARKEN, THE WAY IS OPEN—I, MICHAEL, CALL ON THEE! 262-27

That same month, eighteen members of group were present and asked for clarification on a statement that Edgar Cayce had made in the same reading, "the scepter has not departed from Israel." They also asked about the difference between Michael being the "Lord of the Way" and the Christ showing the Way. After Cayce responded to both questions, the archangel spoke again. The question, answers and the archangel's response follow:

> (Q) What should be understood by the statement, "the scepter has not departed from Israel?"
> (A) Israel is the chosen of the Lord, and that His promise, His care, His love, has not departed from those that seek to know His way, that seek to see His face, that would draw nigh unto Him. *This* is the meaning, this should be the understanding to all. Those that seek are Israel ...
> (Q) What is the relationship between Michael the lord of the way, and Christ the way?
> (A) Michael is an archangel that stands before the throne of the Father. The Christ is the Son, the way *to* the Father, and one that came into the earth as man, the Son of man, that man might have the access to the Father; hence the way. Michael is the lord or the guard of the change that comes in every soul that seeks the way, even as in those periods when His manifestations came in the earth.
>   BOW THINE HEADS, O YE SONS OF MEN, WOULD YE KNOW THE WAY: FOR I, MICHAEL, THE LORD OF THE WAY, WOULD WARN THEE THAT THOU STANDEST NOT IN THE WAY OF THY BROTHER NOR SITTEST IN THE SEATS OF THE SCORNFUL, [Psalm 1:1] BUT RATHER MAKE KNOWN THAT LOVE, THAT GLORY, THAT POWER IN HIS NAME, THAT NONE BE AFRAID; FOR I, MICHAEL, HAVE SPOKEN!   262-28

After the discourse, Gladys Davis noted in the file: "The above reading was so powerfully given that many of us were moved to tears; all were touched deeply."

In October of that same year, group members had gathered for a reading on a lesson called "the Open Door," which was essentially about maintaining an awareness of the divine presence in daily life. Toward the end of the reading, they asked the sleeping Cayce for a group message and, once again, Michael came through:

> (Q) Is there any message for the group as a whole at this time?
> (A) Be patient, long-suffering, bearing one another's burdens. Be joyous in the Lord. Be not tempestuous in manner, thought, act or deed; rather *serving* in humbleness of spirit. Enjoy the labors. Enjoy those things that make for the unison of thought in Him, knowing ye have been called, and that "By *His* power I, as a member of such a group, called to give myself first, called that self may become a channel, called that I as an individual may cooperate with my brother *everywhere* in making known the joyous words of the Lord; "for the Lord is in His holy temple, let all the earth keep silent. Who *is* this Lord? Where is His temple? Know ye not that your bodies are the living temple, holy and acceptable unto Him, would ye walk in His ways?
>
> HARK! O YE CHILDREN OF MEN! BOW THINE HEADS, YE SONS OF MEN: FOR THE GLORY OF THE LORD IS THINE, WILL YE BE FAITHFUL TO THE TRUST THAT IS PUT IN EACH OF YOU! KNOW IN WHOM YE HAVE BELIEVED! KNOW THAT HE IS LORD OF ALL, AND HIS WORD FAILETH NOT TO THEM THAT ARE FAITHFUL DAY BY DAY: FOR I, MICHAEL, WOULD PROTECT THOSE THAT SEEK TO KNOW HIS FACE!   262-29

As she had done previously, Gladys Davis made a note in the file: "Tears, silence and beautiful attunement followed above reading." She also wrote that upon awakening Edgar Cayce said that he had seen a vision during the reading which moved him so powerfully that he was forced to leave the room and spend time alone with himself. According to Gladys, Cayce said that he has seen "each of us as we should be and as we are," which troubled him greatly.

The next lesson explored by the group was entitled "In His Presence," and study group members would have one final encounter with Michael before year's end. When the sleeping Cayce was asked to provide a group message, the archangel spoke:

(Q) Is there a message for the group at this time as a whole?
(A) BOW THINE HEADS, O YE MEN THAT WOULD SEEK HIS
PRESENCE! Be *strong* in His might! Falter not at thine own weak
self! Know that thy redeemer liveth and may THIS DAY MAKE
KNOWN IN THINE OWN HEART HIS PRESENCE ABIDING WITH
THEE! Root from thine body, thine consciousness, aught that
would hinder His entering in; for *He* would sup with thee! Wilt
thou, then, O *man*, make known thine own decisions? Will ye
be one with Him? The way which I guard leads to that of glory
in the might of the Lord. I, Michael, would guide thee. Do not
disobey. Do not falter. Thou knowest the way.   262-33

In 1931, the Association for Research and Enlightenment (A.R.E.)
would officially replace the Association of National Investigators as the
organization that explored and disseminated the Cayce work. A couple
of years later, in a reading given to discuss the second annual membership meeting of A.R.E. and what those attending might procure from
the event, a reading suggested that the real work of the Association and
its ideals and purposes was "to pass on to others that which has been
found to be of help or aid in individuals' experience." In this manner,
the association might eventually become of tremendous aid to even
greater numbers in the material world. It was during this discourse that
the archangel presented himself:
Then, the message that would be given by him, the lord of the Way:

BOW THINE HEADS, O YE CHILDREN OF MEN! FOR THE DAY
OF THE LORD IS NIGH AT HAND! MAKE THINE OWN PATHS
STRAIGHT, IN THAT YE WALK CIRCUMSPECTLY BEFORE THINE
BROTHER, THAT YE PLACE NOT STUMBLING-BLOCKS IN HIS WAY
NOR CAUSE HIM TO ERR IN THAT HE IS SEEKING TO FIND HIS
WAY! LET THE LIGHT THOU HAST SHINE IN A MORE PERFECT
WAY; FOR AS THE DAY DRAWS NEAR WHEN ALL MUST BE TRIED
SO AS BY FIRE, FIND SELF ON THAT SIDE WHEREIN THINE BROTH-
ER HAS BEEN AIDED!   254-66

In June of 1933, the original study group was working on the lesson
entitled "Love." The lesson was the twelfth in the series and emphasized

that God was essentially love and that an ultimate purpose for each individual was to find ways to manifest that love to all others in their daily
lives. During a discourse on that topic, a reading offered the following:

> In manifesting that love as He has shown, just be kind one to
> another; not in vainglorying, not in hardness of heart. Rather
> in the little things that bespeak of a mind that oft speaks with
> Him. Not in that which would make for vainglory, but rather that
> takes hold on the things that are oft despised of men yet shows
> forth the love of the Father for His children. For, as the father
> pitieth the children, so does the heavenly Father have mercy on
> those that would glory in Him.
>
> COME YE, MY CHILDREN, IN THAT YE HAVE ALL BEEN CALLED
> UNTO THAT WAY WHICH WOULD SHOW FORTH TO THY NEIGH-
> BOR, THY BRETHREN, THAT THE FATHER LOVETH HIS CHILDREN.
> WHO ARE HIS CHILDREN? THEY THAT KEEP HIS COMMAND-
> MENTS DAY BY DAY. FOR, UNTO HIM THAT IS FAITHFUL AND
> TRUE IS GIVEN THE CROWN OF LIFE. THE HARVEST IS RIPE, THE
> LABORERS ARE FEW. BE NOT WEARY BECAUSE THERE HAS BEEN
> THAT WHICH HAS SEEMED TO TROUBLE THEE, FOR THE WAYS
> ARE BEING OPENED TO THOSE THAT SHOW THEMSELVES FAITH-
> FUL AND TRUE. FAINT NOT, FOR THE DAY OF THE LORD IS NEAR
> AT HAND.   262-47

The group would hear from the archangel one more time the following year when they were working on the lessons, "God, The Father, and
His Manifestations in the Earth" and "Desire." Although Michael would
continue to speak through the sleeping Cayce, it would not be during
a formal study group reading. The tone of the May 1934 reading was
the same as those which had gone before:

> COME, YE CHILDREN THAT SEEK THE LIGHT! BOW THINE HEADS
> IN PRAISE TO THE SON. FOR, THE WAY FOR EACH OF YOU THAT
> WOULD SEEK HIS FACE IS BEING OPENED BEFORE THEE. THE
> SON OF MAN, THE CHRIST, THY LORD, IS AMONG THEE, EVEN IN
> THINE HEART—IF YE WILL BUT OPEN THE DOOR TO HIM!
>   262-63

The archangel next made a surprising appearance in 1936 while Edgar Cayce was giving a discourse on "the Sources of Psychic Information." As the information had suggested on other occasions, the sleeping Cayce confirmed that as long as an individual had the proper intent and motivation and sought to be helpful through the use of psychic information, it was simply the "manifestations" of soul forces. Obtaining information from other levels of consciousness was, in other words, a natural occurrence for the soul–self that was seeking to be more in attune with its Creator. The reading advised how an individual could discern whether his or her intent was spiritually motivated with the following:

> If ye would know Him let thy life and thy experience be that thy deeds and thy acts are the fruits of the spirit of truth. Against these there is no law. Love, justice, mercy, peace, brotherly love, kindness, these come from the throne of grace, and thine experience of the soul may be from such. But seekest thou that ye may lord thine self above thine brother, above thine neighbor, the answers come only from those sources, those souls that have forsaken His way.

At that point, Michael spoke:

> Come, my children. Bow thine heads. Call ye on the *Lord* while He may be found; for in *His* day there shall be peace and glory and harmony and brotherly love. Seek to know Him, and that thou receivest in thine experiences—as ye approach through all those channels that may attune themselves to the throne of grace—will be the knowledge and understanding that, "As ye do it unto the least of these, my little ones, ye do it unto me."
>
> 5752-6

Aside from communicating through the study group readings, early in 1940 a young girl known as "the little prophetess" received a life reading from Edgar Cayce. The child had gained a great deal of notoriety for her ability to speak prophetic messages that were published in a regular Pennsylvania newspaper column starting when the child was only four! Cayce outlined a series of lifetimes for the child when she had been involved in the early Church, said that she was truly attuned to things of a spiritual nature, including the "music of the spheres," and counseled the parents:

"Give ye—each one—thanks and praise to thy Maker, through the Christ, the Lord, that ye have been counted worthy to come into the presence of one so endeared to the heart of God, as to have given into thy keeping such a messenger, such a way of manifesting His love in the earth!

Shortly thereafter Michael came through; it had been nearly six years since the archangel's last appearance. It was later discovered that the parents were on the verge of divorce and the child would end up in the custody of her father, who did not approve of her prophetic utterances. The little prophetess would soon cease her work with prophecy entirely. Toward the end of the reading when the question was asked, "Anything else?" The response came:

Anything else?!! *Worlds*! Worlds might be filled with that as might be given! But let each of you here so live the Christ-Consciousness, as manifested in the Master, that you may be counted worthy to be even as those who would gather the crumbs of wisdom that will be manifested through this entity!
 HARK! YE FRIENDS! I, MICHAEL, LORD OF THE WAY, WOULD GIVE THEE WARNING! BOW THINE HEADS, YE VILE ONES OF THE EARTH! KNOW WHAT HAS BEEN ENTRUSTED TO THEE! LIVE THE LIFE, LEST YE BE COUNTED ACCURSED FOR BEING UNWORTHY OF THE TRUST GIVEN THEE!   2156-2

The archangel Michael's next appearance came in November 1940 while Cayce was giving a reading on the potential for oil in Smith County, Texas. Several individual were part of a corporation that held leases on three thousand acres in the area. Earlier, the readings had confirmed the presence of large fields of oil, but the oil had proven hard to reach by conventional drilling methods. It was during a follow-up reading in which the individuals sought assistance to overcome some of these problems with their search that Michael came through and essentially scolded the group for using Cayce's psychic talents for anything other than "man's search for God":

> COME! HARKEN YE CHILDREN OF MEN! BOW THINE HEADS, YE SONS OF MEN! FOR I, MICHAEL, WOULD SPEAK WITH THEE CONCERNING THOSE THINGS YE QUESTION HERE! HAVE YE NOT SEEN AND HEARD—UPON THE COURSE THAT IS PURSUED IN THE SEARCH THROUGH THIS MAN FOR KNOWLEDGE—IN SUCH YE DEVIATE AT THAT DEVELOPMENT OF MATERIALITY IN MAN'S SEARCH FOR GOD?   1561-19

Michael would make one final appearance six months before Edgar Cayce would give his last reading for himself. The date was March 14, 1944. Edgar Cayce would give his last reading in September 1944, just prior to having a stroke. He would subsequently die on January 3, 1945. The March reading was in response to Cayce's failing health. He had been having problems with a cold and congestion and was on the verge of pneumonia. Nine individuals were present for the reading—all anxiously hoping that Edgar Cayce might be able to somehow rejuvenate himself.

As had frequently occurred in Cayce's life, the reading suggested that he needed more balance and consistency in life—physically, mentally, and spiritually. It also suggested that his own emotions and state of mind were part of his present physical challenges. It encouraged him to keep his body alkaline—eating foods that would cultivate an alkaline response. It recommended that he also take a walk in the open air each day for exercise. The reading then offered the following spiritual advice:

> Don't preach, don't act in one direction and then say or do those things in another direction.
>> Be patient with those who are weak.
>> Be kind to those who are even ugly.
>> Be gentle with those activities wherein there is the necessity that ye live consistently, that ye be consistent with that ye would represent among thy fellow men.
>> For know, the Lord is in His holy temple. If thou hast, as His

child, desecrated thy temple—in word, in act, in deed—know that ye alone may make those corrections, and that thy body is the temple of the living God. Act as though it were, and not as if it were a pigpen or a place of garbage for the activities of others. Then keep thy body, thy mind, wholly in an active service for thy Lord.

It was then that those present heard Michael come through; his voice reverberating throughout the room in which they sat.

BOW THINE HEADS, YE CHILDREN OF MEN! FOR I, MICHAEL, LORD OF THE WAY, WOULD SPEAK WITH THEE! YE GENERATION OF VIPERS, YE ADULTEROUS GENERATION, BE WARNED!
THERE IS TODAY BEFORE THEE GOOD AND EVIL! CHOOSE THOU WHOM YE WILL SERVE!
WALK IN THE WAY OF THE LORD! OR ELSE THERE WILL COME THAT SUDDEN RECKONING, AS YE HAVE SEEN!
BOW THINE HEADS, YE WHO ARE UNGRACIOUS, UNREPEN-TANT! FOR THE GLORY OF THE LORD IS AT HAND!
THE OPPORTUNITY IS BEFORE THEE! ACCEPT OR REJECT!
But don't be *pigs*!   294-208

A couple of weeks later, one of Edgar Cayce's supporters asked him what he thought the warning from Michael was all about. In his letter, Cayce admitted that he was somewhat "afraid to try to answer" the question. He referred the woman to the Book of Jude, part of which details periods in the history of humankind when individuals warred with one another, spoke evil of those things that were sacred, and details how Michael struggled with Satan over the body of Moses [Jude 1:9], Cayce suggested that it may have been an encouragement for all those present (including himself) to truly live up to that they claimed to believe keeping true to "the whole law; the spiritual law." (Report 2072-13)

The archangel Michael was not heard from again.

4

The Angels Speak:
Halaliel, the Angel of Karma

For a brief fifteen-month period between October 1933 and January 1935, another angel would make its presence known through the unconscious Edgar Cayce. According to those present, however, unlike the encounters with the archangel Michael, in all of these experiences Edgar Cayce maintained his normal voice and inflection. During the first visit, the voice identified itself simply as Halaliel and claimed that he was one who had fought during the biblical Fall against those who had separated themselves from the Creator. In other words, this angelic messenger suggested that he had been on the side of light while others had instead chosen separation and darkness.

Keeping in mind that the core premise of the study group information is to assist individuals in manifesting the Christ Consciousness in the earth, which was defined as "the awareness of the soul's oneness with God," Halaliel's appearance would eventually cause some measure of disagreement among study group members. Most members of the group wanted to remain true to the original focus of aligning with the

Oneness consciousness that had been prescribed by the readings; others thought that the opportunity to obtain information directly from the angelic realms was not something they should easily ignore.

The timing of Halaliel's appearance coincided perfectly with the material being examined by the readings, as his first visitation occurred on October 15, 1933, while Study Group #1 was exploring the lesson entitled "Day and Night." That lesson deals, in part, with the story of Creation, each soul's struggle between those things of the spirit versus those things of the material world, and the fact that, ultimately, we take with us into our subsequent incarnations the awareness we have gained applying the laws of the Creator in the material world. The goal is that each individual will eventually become cognizant of the soul's oneness with God, effectively regaining what was lost during the biblical Fall.

Members of Study Group #1 listened closely as Cayce described how a soul could actually grow in awareness by being separated from the light, for it would then subsequently choose to be more in alignment with the source of its Creation. The reading explained how the process of reincarnation was designed to prompt the evolution of both mind and soul as individuals experienced various lifetimes in the earth. After a number of group members had asked for and received personal messages, a general question was asked encouraging Cayce to explain "the existence of darkness before the existence of light." The answer included, in part:

> ... He has not willed that any soul should perish, but from the beginning has prepared a way of escape! What, then, is the meaning of the separation? Bringing into being the various phases that the soul may find in its manifested forms the consciousness and awareness of its separation, and itself, by that through which it passes in all the various spheres of its awareness. Hence the separation, and light and darkness. Darkness, that it had separated—that a soul had separated itself from the light. Hence He called into being Light, that the awareness began ...all souls in the beginning were one with the Father. The separation, or turning away, brought evil. Then there became the necessity of the awareness of self's being out of accord with, or out of the realm of blessedness; and, as given of the Son, "yet

learned he obedience through the things which he suffered."
262-56

It was then that Halaliel came through and introduced himself:

Come, my children! Ye no doubt have gained from the comment this day a new initiate has spoken in or through this channel; Halaliel, that was with those in the beginning who warred with those that separated themselves and became as naught.

No further information was given because Cayce awoke immediately after Halaliel's statement. It was nine days later, while Edgar Cayce was procuring additional information for a lecture and paper on the topic of how things of the spirit could impact things of the material world, that a reading suggested those present ask individuals in spirit (including Halaliel) for their perspective. (5756–10) A subsequent reading was given that same afternoon. Although Halaliel did not speak during the course of the reading, the information suggested that Halaliel was present in the room. When Edgar Cayce awoke, he said that he would "like to always feel surrounded by as helpful influences" as he had at the time.

Overall, the reading was about the fact that when spiritual beings first entered the earth, they inadvertently separated themselves from the consciousness of God. Since that time, spirit had continued to move over the face of the earth in an attempt to reawaken each soul to its awareness of divine consciousness. Because the material world was simply a "shadow" of the soul's divine nature, that movement of spirit had often resulted in all kinds of misunderstandings and partial un-derstandings of humanity's connection to God. Over time, everything from worshipping the sun to a true understanding of the operation of spirit in the earth had become the result as each soul undertook a personal search to find something it innately felt was missing—the true awareness of its personal connection to the Creator. (5756–11)

On January 7, 1934, study group members gathered for a reading to affirm their understanding of the lesson entitled "Day and Night." The sleeping Cayce affirmed that the group's overall grasp of the material was "very good." It added, however, that since the lesson was about Day and Night and the overall journey of a soul experiencing its connection

with the light (day) versus its separation (night) from the consciousness of the divine, it was important to keep in mind that Spirit would
continually reach out to any who remained separated. Cayce affirmed
that Jesus's parable of the hundred sheep was actually about this very
premise:

> And he spake this parable unto them, saying,
> What man of you, having an hundred sheep, if he lose
> one of them, doth not leave the ninety and nine in the
> wilderness, and go after that which is lost, until he find it?
> And when he hath found it, he layeth it on his shoulders,
> rejoicing.
> And when he cometh home, he calleth together his friends
> and neighbours, saying unto them, Rejoice with me; for I
> have found my sheep which was lost.
> I say unto you, that likewise joy shall be in heaven over
> one sinner that repenteth, more than over ninety and nine
> just persons, which need no repentance.   Luke 15:3-7

The reading volunteered the fact that the next lesson would cover
the subject "God, the Father, and His manifestations in the earth." When
it concluded with that discussion, group members asked the following
question: "Who is Halaliel, the one who gave us a message on Oct. 15th?"
Cayce responded that Halaliel was one who had fought on the side of
the light when "there was the rebellion in heaven." (262-57)

The very next day during a reading given to a forty-five-year-old
woman interested in theosophy, psychic development, and spirit guides,
Cayce stated that each individual in the earth could obtain guidance
from as high a source as desired, whether it was from an individual
soul or from the cosmic consciousness. When the woman asked, "how
high is this source?" in terms of the information coming through, the
answer came: "From the universal forces, and as emanated through the
teacher that gives same—as one that has been given—Halaliel." (443-3)

In spite of ill health, Edgar Cayce took a trip to New York to give
readings and visit with some of his supporters. He was just over pneumonia and still had a severe cough and chest pains. Perhaps it was due
to his illness and physical weakness that two weeks later Halaliel made

another appearance. A reading was requested on "the spiritual, mental and physical changes which are coming to the earth." Ironically, excerpts from this reading would be quoted for decades as one of the most cataclysmic readings ever given by Cayce on "earth changes"—most individuals never being aware of the fact that: 1) Edgar Cayce was ill, definitely impacting his intuitive abilities and 2) the source was not Edgar Cayce but instead Halaliel, who would eventually become known by students of the Cayce material as the "angel of karma." The two most catastrophic statements of things to come included:

As to the changes physical again: The earth will be broken up in the western portion of America. The greater portion of Japan must go into the sea. The upper portion of Europe will be changed as in the twinkling of an eye. Land will appear off the east coast of America. There will be the upheavals in the Arctic and in the Antarctic that will make for the eruption of volcanos in the Torrid areas, and there will be shifting then of the poles—so that where there has been those of a frigid or the semi-tropical will become the more tropical, and moss and fern will grow. And these will begin in those periods in '58 to '98, when these will be proclaimed as the periods when His light will be seen again in the clouds ...

And, after the question, "What are the world changes to come this year [1934] physically?" the following:

The earth will be broken up in many places. The early portion will see a change in the physical aspect of the west coast of America. There will be open waters appear in the northern portions of Greenland. There will be new lands seen off the Caribbean Sea, and *dry* land will appear ... South America shall be shaken from the uppermost portion to the end ...

In between these statements, the angel would declare "I, Halaliel, have spoken." (3976-15) Since neither the 1934 nor the 1958–1998 events occurred, was Halaliel describing a possible karmic outcome destined to befall the planet, one that was apparently superseded by other events?

Perhaps such things as outside spiritual influences, the prayers of countless thousands, the events of World War II? The answer is unclear. What is clear, however, is that Halaliel had been wrong.

The following month while still in New York, Edgar Cayce was meeting with Irish medium and parapsychologist Eileen Garrett (1893–1970) at the home of a mutual friend. The two were contemporaries and very familiar with each other's work. Edgar Cayce had often stated that the source of his information was the Akashic Records and that his superconscious mind was somehow able to access this higher level of information. The source of Eileen Garrett's information was a spirit guide named "Uvani." Garrett and Cayce had come together in order for each to give a reading on the other's psychic work, to explore how each had developed the intuitive gift, and to ascertain how that gift was connected to past lives and personal soul development.

Edgar Cayce gave the first reading. He stated that Garrett's psychic ability was a natural byproduct of her own soul development and that generally the source of her information was associated with "influences from . . . teachers, instructors, directors" in the spirit plane attempting to give a better comprehension of soul activity in the material world. In terms of past incarnations that had led to her psychic gifts, the reading suggested that the strongest influence had come from a Persian lifetime during the Zoroastrian period when Garrett had been a teacher skilled at awakening within individuals their relationship with the "spiritual realms." In terms of recommendations, the sleeping Cayce suggested that as long as Garrett remained true to her spiritual ideals and up-held her desire to be constructive in assisting all those who sought to know "the mysteries of soul and self-development," she would remain a helpful channel. At the end of the reading the question was asked, "What entity is giving this information now?" The response came: "Being directed, as has been indicated, from the [Akashic] records through Halaliel." (507-1)

Later that afternoon it was Eileen Garrett's turn to give a reading on Edgar Cayce. Once Garrett was in the unconscious state her guide came through and announced himself: "It is I, Uvani, I give you greeting, friends. Peace be with you . . . " Uvani stated that Cayce had the ability to set aside his own consciousness and travel to the "etheric state." It was a process, Uvani suggested, that created a tremendous drain on Cayce's physical body to such an extent that he was inevitably giving "something of his own life" during the reading's process. In Uvani's words: "he is using his own light, he is dimming his own light." It was for that reason that Uvani suggested he could assist Edgar Cayce by finding a channel in the spirit plane to help with the readings. In terms of past lives that had facilitated Cayce's psychic prowess, Uvani mentioned Egypt, Persia, and India. Uvani went on to suggest again that he could secure a spirit "helper" for Cayce on the other side, lessening the strain on Cayce's physical body. Uvani added that this help would give Cayce "a virility, an ease, and immediately a greater peace of mind." Toward the end of the reading the question was asked, "Do you connect in any way with . . . the name Halaliel?" Uvani's response was that Halaliel was "one who has been scorched, one who has overcome, one who has survived." (Report 507-1)

Apparently, the possibility of working with a spirit guide was discussed among Edgar Cayce, his son, Hugh Lynn, and his secretary, Gladys, after Eileen Garrett left. Three days later, while still staying in New York, another reading was procured regarding Cayce's psychic work and how it might be of "the greatest possible service to mankind." After the reading discussed the ongoing work and its purpose to help all of humankind find a closer walk with God, the following question was asked:

> You will consider the sitting with Mrs. Eileen Garrett, held in this room, on the afternoon of Feb. 3, 1934, together with the information and suggestions given by Uvani, her alleged control. Would it be advisable for Edgar Cayce to follow her suggestions as to seeking assistance from the entity described whom Uvani claims will increase the coherence and power of the readings?

The response suggested that there was no higher source of information available than that which Edgar Cayce was already using. The answer came: "Does Uvani claim to know better than the Master who made him?" (254-71)

Over the next few months Cayce went back to giving readings as normal. Most of the individuals who obtained readings sought help with their physical health. Additional readings were given on spiritual lessons to the study group as well as on meditation and prayer to a healing prayer group that involved some of the same members. Other individuals also procured readings on past lives, with the focus being on what lessons still needed to be learned by the soul as well as how past–life influences created a reservoir of memory that affected individuals in terms of both relationships and vocation.

During the months of May and July 1934, respectively, two additional readings on the topic of spirit communication were requested. Both were somewhat disjointed. The first may have included a variety of outside influences, including Halaliel, that were trying to speak through the sleeping Cayce, but after only a minute Cayce suggested that the collective intent was not unified, and he ended very quickly with: "We are through. We must turn back." (5756–12)

The second attempt was much longer—lasting nearly forty–five minutes—but it was even more confusing. Cayce began by stating that with spirit communication it was important to realize "the soul lives on" and that deceased individuals retained their personalities, individualities, beliefs, etc., for a time after making the transition to the other side. In fact, on another occasion, a reading would make the point even more clear:

> For do not consider for a moment … that an individual soul-entity passing from an earth plane as a Catholic, a Methodist, an Episcopalian, is something else because he is dead! He's only a dead Episcopalian, Catholic or Methodist. And such personalities and their attempts are the same …   254-92

In other words, those present were being called to understand that death does not bring instant enlightenment and just because something came from the spirit world does not mean that it is accurate. The analogy might be, "Why would you listen to something from your deceased Uncle Joe now any more than you would have listened to him when he was alive?"

After this explanation, several deceased individuals from Cayce's extended family seemed to clamor to speak. The sleeping Cayce apparently heard each of them and provided his half of the conversation. Those individuals included Edgar Cayce's deceased mother, Dr. Thomas House (the original physician from the Cayce hospital), Cayce's grandmother, Milton Porter Cayce (the child that Edgar and his wife, Gertrude, had lost as an infant), and an Uncle Joel. At one point, the angelic presence again identified itself with, "This is Halaliel speaking." When Gladys Davis asked if she could have a message from her deceased father, the reply was: " . . . Not at present here; he is speaking with another . . . " (5749-14) The reading ended.

In September 1934, the original study group was obtaining a reading on the lesson of "Desire." Perhaps, ironically, halfway through the reading the statement came that it was essentially due to the collective desire of the group that Halaliel had made his appearance in the first place:

> *To all we would give*: Be patient. That part thou hast chosen in such a work is born of truth. Let it come in and be a part of thy daily life. Look in upon the experiences, for, as will be seen, my children, there has been appointed one that may aid thee in thy future lessons, and he will be thy teacher, thy guide, [Halaliel?] one sent through the power of thine own desires. Thine own selves, then, may present his being, meeting, living, dwelling, with thee. Not the Christ, but His messenger, with the Christ from the beginning, and is to other worlds what the Christ is to this earth.   262-71

The offer caused group members to seek further clarification two weeks later when they next gathered for a reading. After a brief discussion on their overall understanding of the "Desire" lesson and the fact that it was "very good," the question was asked: "Please explain, so that we may all understand, just what was meant in the last reading, as to the help to be given on the lessons, what we should do, what our approach should be?"

The answer suggested that each member of the group had a choice to make. One choice was continuing to work with the study group information as they had been doing—each individual applying the lessons until they became personally understood. This was the path offered by the Christ in which each individual was willing to become a " . . . channel of blessing to someone else . . . " The other choice was to let Halaliel guide the lessons in which they would not really be about personal application or about becoming a channel to someone else; instead, this approach would make the lessons " . . . change to a more informative nature . . . " (262-72)

Members of the group discussed the choice over the next month. Although the majority wanted to continue working with the information as they had been doing—the approach that seemed to be favored by the Christ—two or three members of the group hoped that they could continue their work with *both* sources. When the group procured their next reading in October, the reading encouraged them to instead choose the path of the Christ:

> . . . The Master has called, and His love will protect thee if thou wilt in thy daily life live that thou hast given thy brother, thy friend, as a guide, as an example!
>
> So, as ye choose, know that lesson thou hast been given becomes a part of thee—thy Destiny! For ye as souls, as individuals, are *building* same . . .   262-73

In spite of this encouragement, some group members remained torn. The idea of having an ongoing dialogue with the angelic realms was apparently too appealing to pass up. The readings gave their final encouragement the following January:

> What, then, is thy Destiny? It is made in that thou pervertest not that thou *knowest* to do in thine heart respecting thy fellow man! For ye look to Him who is the author and the finisher of faith. He *is* Faith, *and* Truth, *and* Light - *and* in no other is there comeliness at all. For He is the rock of salvation; the bright, the morning star; the rose of Sharon; the *wonderful* counsellor. In Him *is* thy Destiny. Turn ye not away from Him. [Gladys Davis made a notation in the reading: 'Again warning not to accept Halaliel or any other.']

Even with this advice, one of the group members remained uncertain and asked why they should believe that accepting Halaliel would not enable them to receive " . . . the highest . . . guided by the Spirit of Truth?"

The answer was short and to the point: "It has been given." (262–75)

The voice of Halaliel was not heard from again. However, an extremely interesting reading occurred the following month when Edgar Cayce had gone to Washington, DC to meet with an individual who wanted to be hired as manager of the Cayce work. The individual, Mr. [699], was also extremely interested in spirit guides and wanted to know how these guides influenced the Cayce readings. It was during this reading that Halaliel was described as one " . . . who has made the ways that have been heavy—but as the means for the *understanding*." In other words, Halaliel oversaw challenges and hardships that could lead to a growth in personal awareness, suggesting that his identity was in fact "the angel of karma."

The series of questions asked by Mr. [699] and Cayce's responses follow:

> (Q) For the better and more rational presentation of the work of Edgar Cayce to the world, will you, if you consider same in order, kindly inform us of Thine Identity and the source or sources from which you bring us the information given in answer to our questions in the readings other than the Physical? Is it from the Astral—
>
> (A) (interrupting) From the universal forces that are acceptable and accessible to those that in earnestness *open* their minds, their souls, to the wonderful words of truth and light.
>
> (Q) To what extent are the Masters of the Great White Brotherhood directing the activities of Edgar Cayce? Who are the Masters directly in charge?
>
> (A) *Messengers* from the higher forces that may manifest from the Throne of grace itself.
>
> (Q) Who are the Masters directly in charge? Is Saint Germain—
>
> (A) (Interrupting) Those that are directed by the Lord of lords, the King of kings, Him that came that ye might be one with the Father.
>
> (Q) Is Saint Germain among them? Who is Halaliel?
>
> (A) These are all but messengers of the Most High. Halaliel is the one who from the beginning has been a leader of the heavenly host, who has defied Ariel, who has made the ways that have

been heavy—but as the means for the *understanding*. [Isaiah 29th chapter?]

(Q) Is Saint Germain among them?

(A) When needed.

(Q) Please give us Thine Identity?

(A) He that seeks that has not gained control seeks damnation to his own soul! Control thine inner self that *ye* may *know* the true life and light! for he that would name the Name must have become perfect in himself!

(Q) If Mr. Cayce is a member and a messenger of the Great White Brotherhood, how do the Masters wish him to proceed and should not his activities henceforth be presented as Their Work?

(A) As the work of the *master* of masters, that may be presented when in those lines, those accords necessary through the White Brotherhood. This—this—*this,* my friends, even but *limits;* while in Him is the Whole. Would thou make of thyself, of w, a limited means of activity? Would thou seek to be hindered by those things that have made of many contending forces that continue to war one with another even in the air, even in the elemental forces? For He, thy Lord, thy God, hath called thee by name, even as He has given, "Whosoever will drink the cup, even as of my blood, he may indeed be free." While ye labor, let *Him* that is the author, that is the finisher, that is the Life, that is the bread of life, that is the blood of life, let *Him* alone be thy guide! Dost He call any soul into service, *then* by name will He—does He— designate, and to whom it becomes a charge to keep—even as he has walked with Him, this body that ye use as a channel of approach to the Throne; ye make of same oft as a laughingstock to thy very soul through thine own selfishness! Let the light of Him, thy Christ, thy God, *in,* that it may cleanse thy body, that it may lighten thy soul, that it may purge thy mind, that ye will only be just gentle, just kind; not find fault with any, for with faults ye build *barriers* to thine own soul's enlightenment. "I, thy God, thy Christ, beseech thee!"   254-83

Forty years later, Hugh Lynn Cayce, Edgar Cayce's eldest son and a member of the original study group, sent a memo to Gladys Davis

Turner about his recollection of the group's experience with Halaliel. Gladys had requested the memo for the archives. Hugh Lynn's response, dated December 6, 1975, was as follows:

> Beginning October 15, 1933, and continuing for a number of months members of Search for God Group #1 went through a rather difficult decision-making period. This occurred during a time when there was great economic difficulty during the so-called depression years and during this time Edgar Cayce experienced a period of ill health.
>
> It should be pointed out here that this is a personal opinion, but it is also an opinion which was held by all the members of Group #1 with the exception of two members who simply raised questions about the possibility of having both the guidance which was suggested and, what all agreed, was a higher attunement with the ideals related to the Christ Consciousness. It was for all a period of questioning, testing, and decision making.
>
> Though Edgar Cayce still maintained his voice and his manner, inflection, etc., the statement was made that a character known as Halaliel could direct the material to be given in the readings in a clearer more organized fashion. It was indicated that a decision needed to be made as to whether this offer of clarification could be accepted by the group ... Over a period of several readings as indicated here, and after considerable discussion at the study group meetings a large proportion of Group #1 felt that the purposes and guidance for the group's activities should continue to be focused toward the level of the Christ Consciousness and that the offer of clarification and direction should not be accepted.
>
> As I understand the readings which followed, the group was commended for the choice and stand which had been taken.
>
> On one occasion following a reading with Eileen Garrett [507-1, 2/3/34] her control, Uvani, offered to clarify the readings, and a question was asked in reading 254-71 [2/6/34] as to whether this would be a wise idea or not. Again, the offer was not accepted here because of a statement in the reading itself. I think this is a similar kind of diversion brought on by the stress

and trial through which the whole group, as well as the nation, was passing and because of the physical disturbances Edgar Cayce suffered at the time.—Hugh Lynn Cayce

It may be interesting to note that the original study group did complete the series of twenty-four lessons outlined by the Edgar Cayce readings and eventually published those lessons as *A Search for God,* Books I and II. Those lessons became the core transformational materials used by Edgar Cayce's A.R.E. ever since, resulting in literally thousands of study groups and foreign translations of the material around the globe. For decades, countless individuals have claimed that the study group information compiled by that original group has transformed their lives and given then a closer walk with God, effectively confirming the original promise that had come from the Archangel Michael in 1932:

...YOU THAT HAVE BEEN CHOSEN FOR A SERVICE IN THIS PERIOD WHEN THERE IS THE NEED OF THAT SPIRIT BEING MADE MANIFEST IN THE EARTH, THAT THE WAY MAY BE KNOWN TO THOSE THAT SEEK THE LIGHT! ...   262-27

5

The Readings' Addendum to Biblical Accounts of Angelic Encounters

The Bible discusses the appearance, intercession, and communicative role of angels on hundreds of occasions. These divine beings often serve as messengers, responsible for bringing spiritual insights, warnings, guidance, and even aid into the material world. Throughout his life, Edgar Cayce had a strong interest in the Bible and made a personal a commitment to reading it from cover to cover regularly. It is therefore not surprising that the readings often explored biblical stories in greater detail, including a number of instances when additional insights into some of the biblical accounts of angelic intercession were provided.

In 1925, it was the patronage of stockbroker and businessman Morton Blumenthal who made it possible for the Cayce family to move from Dayton, Ohio to Virginia Beach, Virginia. Thereafter, the readings repeatedly assured Edgar Cayce that his work would spread from the then small town of Virginia Beach to help countless people: "first to the

individuals, [then to the groups,] then to the classes, then to the masses."
(2091-2) Morton and his brother, Edwin, underwrote the construction of
the hospital, the establishment of Atlantic University, and provided ongoing support to Edgar Cayce and his family. Unfortunately, due to the
Great Depression, petty jealousies, and being financially overextended,
within six years of the move Morton withdrew support from the Cayce
work, leaving the Cayce family financially strapped and abandoned in
Virginia Beach. It would become a time of great anxiety and inner soul
searching for Edgar Cayce.

This unexpected turn of events seemed to be foreshadowed in a
dream that Cayce's wife, Gertrude, had in 1926. Gertrude recalled the
dream, as follows: "October 8, 1926, dream regarding Morton Blumenthal visiting us and wanting us to move into a small place of two or
three very small rooms of a cottage belonging to someone else, of me
getting mad or hurt and crying." During a personal reading, Gertrude
asked for an interpretation of the dream. Cayce provided the following:

> In this there are presented conditions, as it were, of a forecast
> of conditions as will arise ... Then the use of the knowledge as
> is gained through such dreams may be applied in the life of
> the entity in such a way and manner as being forewarned, be
> forearmed ...   538-22

Years later, Gladys Davis would make the following notation in the
archives: "On 6/31, Mrs. Cayce and her family were evicted by Mr.
Blumenthal and were for a time crowded into very small quarters." It
was this very situation—losing the hospital, being financially strapped,
and having a great deal of uncertainty about permanent housing or
the location of that housing—that lay at the heart of Edgar Cayce's
personal challenges.

In terms of dreams, the Cayce readings explored approximately 900
dreams for a variety of individuals and affirmed that dreams could be
a primary source of personal guidance. The challenge, however, is that
most individuals do not attempt to remember their dreams. Nonethe-
less, the readings assert that dreams can explore every aspect of personal life: health, relationships, financial advice, answers to problems
facing the waking mind, prophetic insights into one's personal future,

even information regarding past lives. It is this last component that was at the heart of one of Edgar Cayce's own dreams about a past-life experience that gave an addendum to an Old Testament account of angelic intercession.

As background information, it may be important to point out the readings' premise as to why past-life dreams occur in the first place. Cayce maintained that these dreams generally take place not because of the past but because the information is somehow connected to the present. Individuals receive past-life information in dreams because they are encountering something in their present experience that is similar to something that happened previously to them. Oftentimes that something is a relationship that is about to reappear, or it may be an experience from a past life that is about to reoccur. It was the past's similarities with a present-day experience that seemed to prompt one of Edgar Cayce's past-life dreams.

At the time, Cayce was still reeling from his break with the Blumenthals. His lifelong dream of the hospital had come to an end. There were ongoing worries about the family's financial stability and—after being evicted by the Blumenthals—having to move to a small rental house. Afterwards, they had the reoccurring experience of renting a small house, only to have it sold out from under them and having to move again. Cayce couldn't help but wonder whether or not they were even supposed to remain in Virginia Beach. Their search for "permanent quarters" in which to move and make a home would last almost a year. The whole experience was a tremendous burden, personal trial, and truly a time of private anguish for Edgar Cayce. It was in the midst of all this that Cayce recalled the following dream in February 1932:

> I thought I was with Mr. and Mrs. Lot and their two daughters running out of Sodom when it was raining fire and brimstone. What had been called, "she turned to a pillar of salt," [Gen. 19:26] because she looked back, was that they really passed through the heat—as came from the fire from heaven, and all were tried as by that. I got through the fire.

Although Cayce seemed intrigued by the fact that the dream was suggesting Lot's wife had turned into a pile of dust (not salt) because of the tremendous heat, he wanted to know why the dream had occurred in the first place, and he asked in a reading to provide additional insights.

The reading's response came as a complete surprise for it stated unequivocally that Cayce had been one of the individuals who had accompanied Lot, his wife, and his two daughters out of Sodom: " . . . this is rather as an experience through which the body passed with those at the period; for the body then, the entity, was one that accompanied these bodies in this experience, and that in the present he was also undergoing what might be called 'trials . . . by fire.'" (294-136) In other words, his present problems of being trialed by fire had reawakened an awareness of this past-life experience. The reading added that Cayce's success in making it through his present challenges was dependent upon his "attitude and activities." Gertrude asked for further clarification: "Did the body [Edgar Cayce] actually live at that period as a physical entity?" Her husband responded: "As given, one of those sent as the warning, or warner to the people, as to what was coming to pass."

Turning to the Bible, the story of Lot is examined in the Book of Genesis in portions of chapters 11 through 14 and all of chapter 19. A summary of the biblical account relevant to Cayce's dream follows:

As noted previously (see preface), three "angels" disguised as mortal men appeared to Abraham and correctly predicted that he and his wife Sarah would have a son. This is relevant to the story of Lot because Abraham was Lot's uncle (Abraham would plead with God to save the wicked city of Sodom) and, according to the Bible, two of those three angelic messengers would next journey to Sodom to warn Lot and his family of the destruction that was about to befall their city. (Gen. 18:22 and Gen. 19:1) Although not immediately recognizing the two travelers upon their arrival as angels, Lot opened his house to them, encouraged them to rest and wash their feet, and prepared a feast for them to enjoy.

Apparently, news of the men's arrival spread throughout the city, and before they could fall asleep, a gang of young men and old approached Lot's house and demanded that the visitors be turned over for their sexual pleasure: "Where are the men which came in to thee this night? bring them out unto us, that we may know them." (Gen. 19:5) In order to protect Lot and his family, the two visitors revealed that they had superhuman abilities by striking the gang with such power that all the men were blinded. The angels encouraged Lot and his family to leave as quickly as possible, but Lot was apparently too slow and seemed to linger in confusion as to what to do next. The angels took hold of Lot and his family and transported the four of them beyond the city limits: "And while he lingered, the men laid hold upon his hand, and upon the hand of his wife, and upon the hand of his two daughters . . . and they brought him forth, and set him without the city." (Gen. 19:16) As the city became engulfed in flames, Lot's wife turned back and became a pillar of salt [ash?]. (Gen. 19:26) Afterward, Lot had to decide where he and his daughters were supposed to live. Because of his personal fears, he withdrew from the city and chose instead to live in the mountains of Zoar. (Gen. 19:30) That is the essential story.

Cayce's dream suggested and the readings confirmed that Edgar Cayce had literally been one of the messengers sent to warn Lot and his family. Unfortunately, no further details on that specific incarnation were ever requested, so we are left with at least two distinct possibilities about the nature of that lifetime.

The first possibility is that Cayce had essentially been a "spirit guide" to Lot and his family. Not physical, he may have been able to draw upon spiritual gifts that caused Lot to surmise that he was an angelic messenger. The second is that this appearance as a messenger corresponded with a literal past life in which Cayce somehow possessed superhuman abilities. Although it could have been an incarnation never specifically detailed in the readings, the late W.H. Church, Cayce scholar and writer, suggested that the appearance corresponded to the same period in history when Edgar Cayce had lived as an Egyptian High Priest named Ra–Ta and that it was Ra–Ta who had briefly deserted his essential leadership responsibilities in accepting the role of divine messenger at that time.[17] Interesting enough, the readings affirm the possibility of this likelihood, as they suggest Ra–Ta was not as confined to physical laws as most individuals: " . . . the being [Edgar Cayce's soul] translated in materiality as Ra–Ta . . . from the infinity forces . . . " (5755-1) Regardless of how it occurred, the readings assert that Edgar Cayce was, in fact, one of Lot's angelic messengers.

---

[17]W.H. Church, *The Lives of Edgar Cayce* (Virginia Beach, VA: A.R.E. Press, 1995), 124–33.

The day after the dream interpretation reading, Cayce obtained another reading in which he sought clarification on the similarities between Lot's story and his "present conditions." In addition to the connection between Edgar Cayce and one of the messengers who had warned Lot, the reading stated that there was a corollary between Cayce and Lot in that after a cataclysmic experience each man had to choose where he and his family would live: In the language of the readings, "In that as given of Lot, there was the choice made by Lot as to whether this experience would be among the peoples in the city or those of the plains, or of those of the hills..." Choosing where to live was one of the challenges facing Edgar Cayce and apparently causing a great deal of personal anxiety. The Cayce's had moved to Virginia Beach with Blumenthal's support. Since that support was gone and the hospital was closed, it was only natural to wonder if they should leave the city and go someplace else. The reading advised otherwise:

> ... Believest thou, that thou hast contacted, do contact, those sources from which good may come to self or to others ...? As has been given, tarry ye in Virginia Beach till ye see the powers of those that would bring to a world an understanding of their relationships to same. Then do so.   294-137

At the end of the reading, Gertrude asked, "Any other advice for the body at this time, or counsel?" The answer was reassuring: "Be thou faithful over the few things, and he that is faithful over a few will be made ruler over many."

Edgar Cayce remained faithful and endured the challenges that faced him. He found comfort in the study group readings and in a core group of enthusiasts who supported him and his work. Although constantly seeing the abandoned hospital building that had been lost to him caused him some measure of regret, he remained in the city of Virginia Beach. By the end of May 1932, the Cayce family found a home that they purchased on Arctic Crescent a few blocks from the oceanfront. There Cayce would remain until his death in 1945, and the home would continue as Association (A.R.E.) headquarters until the old Cayce hospital was repurchased for that purpose in 1956.

In terms of additional insights into the Bible, one of the most detailed explorations of history examined by more than a hundred Cayce readings deals with a little-known Jewish sect called the Essenes. It is that information that delves with much greater detail into one of the most well-known biblical accounts of angelic visitations—the story of the Virgin Mary's visit by the archangel Gabriel. The New Testament records the story, as follows:

> And in the sixth month the angel Gabriel was sent from God unto a city of Galilee, named Nazareth,
>
> To a virgin espoused to a man whose name was Joseph, of the house of David; and the virgin's name was Mary.
>
> And the angel came in unto her, and said, Hail, thou that art highly favoured, the Lord is with thee: blessed art thou among women.
>
> And when she saw him, she was troubled at his saying, and cast in her mind what manner of salutation this should be.
>
> And the angel said unto her, Fear not, Mary: for thou hast found favor with God.
>
> And, behold, thou shalt conceive in thy womb, and bring forth a son, and shalt call his name *Jesus*.
>
> He shall be great, and shall be called the Son of the Highest: and the Lord God shall give unto him the throne of his father David:
>
> And he shall reign over the house of Jacob for ever; and of his kingdom there shall be no end.
>
> Then said Mary unto the angel, How shall this be, seeing I know not a man?
>
> And the angel answered and said unto her, The Holy Ghost shall come upon thee, and the power of the Highest shall overshadow thee: therefore also that holy thing which shall be born of thee shall be called the Son of God.
>
> And, behold, thy cousin Elisabeth, she hath also conceived a son in her old age: and this is the sixth month with her, who was called barren.
>
> For with God nothing shall be impossible.
>
> And Mary said, Behold the handmaid of the Lord; be

it unto me according to thy word. And the angel departed
from her.   Luke 1:26-38

Edgar Cayce's story of Mary's choosing and the visitation by the
archangel Gabriel presents a much more detailed overview of persistent
faith by a dedicated group of spiritual adherents than has been remembered by history. From the readings' perspective, the Essene sect not
only committed themselves to the devout pursuit of personal spiritual
growth, but they also collectively understood their role in making the
way possible for the entrance of the long–awaited Messiah to come into
the earth. This sect, which Cayce claimed drew its foundations from
the "school of the prophets" founded by the Old Testament prophet
Elijah, studied scripture, prophecy, astrology, and personal purity. They
labored for generations, raising children to be spiritual devotees in the
material world. It was into this group that Mary was born and would
eventually be chosen as one of the possible pure channels for the great
soul they hoped to attract. In fact, the readings suggest that children
became a part of the Essene spiritual commitment at a very early age,
citing Mary's own involvement as beginning at the age of four. (5749-8)

In 1941, New York author Enid Severy Smith was in the process of
pulling together what would become a thirty–two–page booklet on
the history of the Essenes. During the course of a reading, the question
was asked: "What is the correct meaning of the term 'Essene?'" Cayce
replied, "Expectancy." When further details about the overall purpose
of the booklet were requested, the response came:

> . . . that there is the expectancy of a new order, or a fulfilling of
> or a return to those activities that may bring about the time for
> that redemption of the world . . . Then, this pamphlet or paper
> should give to others an insight as to what and how there was
> the physical, mental and spiritual attitude of that group; as
> to how those individuals so well acted their part, and yet not
> becoming known in that presented. So, this may enable indi-
> viduals and groups to so prepare themselves as to be channels
> through which the more perfect way may be seen.   254-109

The Essene's ongoing commitment to living in accord with spiritual laws took place over many generations. The readings state that the community not only accepted both Jews and Gentiles as converts to their way of life, but they also treated men and women as equals. Women who became a part of the sect so dedicated themselves that they would become known as "Holy Women." In a number of readings, Cayce describes an experience that occurred at Mt. Carmel where there were a dozen young maidens climbing the stairs of the Essene Temple. A young Mary was in the lead when suddenly the angel Gabriel appeared before all those present and selected her as the one who would become the channel for the Messiah. On one occasion, the description was as follows:

> The temple steps—or those that led to the altar, these were called the temple steps. These were those upon which the sun shone as it arose of a morning when there were the first periods of the chosen maidens going to the altar for prayer; as well as for the burning of the incense. On this day, as they mounted the steps all were bathed in the morning sun; which not only made a beautiful picture but clothed all as in purple and gold. As Mary reached the top step, then, then there were the thunder and lightning, and the angel [Gabriel] led the way, taking the child by the hand before the altar. This was the manner of choice, this was the showing of the way; for she led the others on *this* particular day.   5749-8

Other readings describe the same experience. To a woman who was told that she had been one of the young maidens on the steps that day and would become a lifelong companion of Mary, Cayce stated:

> As has been outlined from here, there were those special groups of individuals who had made some preparations for the expected activities that were to come about during that particular period; especially those of the Essenes who had chosen the twelve maidens to indicate their fitness ... This entity, Josie, was close to Mary when the selection was indicated by the shadow or the angel on the stair, at that period of consecration in the temple. This was not the temple in Jerusalem, but the temple

> where those who were consecrated worshiped, or a school—as
> it might be termed—for those who might be channels.
>
> 1010-17

Cayce states that this angelic encounter would not be the only one with Mary. Instead, it would be one of several discussed among members of the Essene community—stories that would follow her for the rest of her life:

> For, remember, many of those—too—were of that questioned group; who had heard of that girl, that lovely wife of Joseph who had been chosen by the angels on the stair; who had heard of what had taken place in the hills where Elizabeth had gone, when there was the visit from the cousin—and as to those things which had also come to pass in her experience. Such stories were whispered from one to another.   5749-15

> (Q) How long was the preparation in progress before Mary was chosen?
> (A) Three years.
> (Q) In what manner was she chosen?
> (A) As they walked up the steps!
> (Q) Was there any appearance of the angel Gabriel in the home?
> (A) In the temple when she was chosen, in the home of Elizabeth when she was made aware of the presence by being again in the presence of the messenger or forerunner. Again to Joseph at the time of their union. Again (by Michael) at the time when the edict [Herod's edict; Matt. 2:16-18] was given.   5749-7

Although this second quote indicates that there were additional angelic encounters when Mary visited her cousin Elizabeth (who would become the mother of John the Baptist), at the time of her wedding with Joseph, and when Herod sought to kill the baby Jesus out of fear that the child would eventually seek to become king, no additional information was ever requested about these experiences.

The readings briefly verify other New Testament tales of angelic experiences, such as when Jesus was fed and comforted by angels after being tempted in the wilderness to not go through with the crucifixion (Matt. 4:1-11; 5749-15), and when a number of those closest to Jesus did, in fact, see angels in the tomb after his resurrection, but no one thought to ask the sleeping Cayce for additional details. In terms of the resurrection experience, the readings state that a number of those closest to Jesus had heard rumors that He had resurrected, they hurried to the tomb to confirm that joyful possibility. It was then that they saw the angels:

> Hence when those of His loved ones and those of His brethren came on that glad morning when the tidings had come to them, those that stood guard heard a fearful noise and saw a light, and—"the stone has been rolled away!" Then they entered into the garden, and there Mary first saw her *risen* Lord. Then came they of His brethren with the faithful women, those that loved His mother, those that were her companions in sorrow, those that were making preparations that the law might be kept that even there might be no desecration of the ground about His tomb. They, too, of His friends, His loved ones, His brethren, saw the angels.   5749-6

One biblical tale that the readings do explore in greater detail deals with the heavenly choir that appeared to the shepherds over the hills of Bethlehem on the occasion of the birth of Jesus. A thirty-nine-year-old man received a reading from Edgar Cayce and was informed that in a previous lifetime he had been among the shepherds who heard that angelic choir: "The entity then, in the name Slocombi . . . In that experience the entity was among the shepherds that were in the hill country, and among those that heard the song of the angels, "Peace on earth, good will to men." (519-1) The scriptural account of the same story is described in Luke:

> And she brought forth her firstborn son, and wrapped him in swaddling clothes, and laid him in a manger; because there was no room for them in the inn.
> And there were in the same country shepherds abiding in the field, keeping watch over their flock by night.

And, lo, the angel of the Lord came upon them, and the glory of the Lord shone round about them: and they were sore afraid.

And the angel said unto them, Fear not: for, behold, I bring you good tidings of great joy, which shall be to all people.

For unto you is born this day in the city of David a Savior, which is Christ the Lord.

And this shall be a sign unto you; Ye shall find the babe wrapped in swaddling clothes, lying in a manger.

And suddenly there was with the angel a multitude of the heavenly host praising God, and saying,

Glory to God in the highest, and on earth peace, good will toward men.

And it came to pass, as the angels were gone away from them into heaven, the shepherds said one to another, Let us now go even unto Bethlehem, and see this thing which is come to pass, which the Lord hath made known unto us.

And they came with haste, and found Mary, and Joseph, and the babe lying in a manger.   Luke 2:7-16

The Cayce information provides a wealth of additional information about the event. For example, the readings suggest that the innkeeper who had told Joseph and Mary that there was "no room" at the inn was actually an Essene and had made preparations for the couple in a nearby stable, as he was concerned that the presence of the rabble crowd in town for the census was not a suitable environment for the birth of the Messiah. The readings also suggest that when some of those at the inn saw the very pregnant Mary with her husband, Joseph, who was nearly twice her age, they laughed and made fun at the couple—a deed for which some would later feel guilty: " . . . Laughter and jeers followed, at the sight of the elderly man with the beautiful girl, his wife, heavy with child." (5749-15)

The Cayce narrative goes on to suggest that not only were the shepherds aware that something truly unique was occurring, but individuals in the inn also became aware of the song and the change in vibration in the air. Many others saw the star as it shone in the sky:

... Necessity demanded that some place be sought—quickly. Then it was found, under the hill, in the stable—above which the shepherds were gathering their flocks into the fold.

There the Savior, the Child was born; who, through the will and the life manifested, became the Savior of the world—that channel through which those of old had been told that the promise would be fulfilled that was made to *Eve;* the arising again of another like unto Moses; and as given to David, the promise was not to depart from that channel. But lower and lower man's concept of needs had fallen.

Then—when hope seemed gone—the herald angels sang. The star appeared, that made the wonderment to the shepherds, that caused the awe and consternation to all of those about the Inn; some making fun, some smitten with conviction that those unkind things said must needs be readjusted in their relationships to things coming to pass.

All were in awe as the brightness of His star appeared and shone, as the music of the spheres brought that joyful choir, *"Peace on Earth! Good Will to Men of Good Faith."*

All felt the vibrations and saw a great light—not only the shepherds above that stable but those in the Inn as well.

To be sure, those conditions were later to be dispelled by the doubters, who told the people that they had been overcome with wine or what not.

Just as the midnight hour came, there was the birth of the Master.   5749-15

Interestingly enough, Cayce stated that not everyone nearby was able to hear the angelic voices, only those whose consciousness was elevated above personal gratification, sensuality, and the boisterousness of their own personalities:

Who heard these, my children? Those that were seeking for the satisfying of their own desires or for the laudation of their own personality? Rather those close to *nature,* to the hours of meditation and prayer, and those that had given expression, "No room in the Inn!" For no inn, no room, could contain that as

> was being given in a manifested form ... Only then to those that
> sought could such a message come, or could there be heard
> the songs of the angels, or that music of the spheres that sang,
> *"Peace on Earth—Good Will to Men!"*   262-103

What may be most surprising about this event, however, is the readings state unequivocally that the angelic choir above the hills of Bethlehem that Holy Night was not a unique event but is instead an occurrence that happens each and every time a child is born into the earth because of the hope and the possibility that the Christ spirit again might be made manifest in that child's life:

> For this, then, is in every birth—the possibilities, the glories, the
> actuating of that influence of that entrance again of god-man
> into the earth that man might know the way ... He may be born
> into thine own consciousness, thine own understanding ...
>   262-103

In a very real sense, both the Edgar Cayce readings and the Bible suggest that angelic messengers of light remain constantly vigilant in their effort to assist and guide the human creature. Generally, Cayce described how this guidance comes in an effort to attend and support each individual on his or her path toward personal enlightenment. But what of those who chose the path of self rather than the path of God? What happens to those who champion selfishness rather than Divine law? From the readings' perspective, even then the angels are there and remain watchful, waiting for their opportunity to help.

6

Edgar Cayce on Fallen Angels, the Antichrist, and the Lower Self

Monotheism is the belief in only one God. Although there may be many names for that God, there is only one. Christianity, Judaism, Islam all hold to this monotheistic principle. That premise is repeatedly expressed in the Old Testament, including in the following: "Hear, O Israel: The Lord our God is one Lord: And thou shalt love the Lord thy God with all thine heart, and with all thy soul, and with all thy might." (Deut. 6:4–5) The same belief is frequently cited in the Quran, such as the statement: "That is Allah, your Lord; there is no deity except Him, the Creator of all things, so worship Him. And He is Disposer of all things." (Quran, Al-An'am 6:102) Jesus calls to mind the very same idea when He is asked about the most important commandment:

> And one of the scribes came, and having heard them rea-
> soning together, and perceiving that he had answered them
> well, asked him, Which is the first commandment of all?
> And Jesus answered him, The first of all the command-

ments is, Hear, O Israel; The Lord our God is one Lord:
And thou shalt love the Lord thy God with all thy heart,
and with all thy soul, and with all thy mind, and with all
thy strength: this is the first commandment.

Mark 12: 28-30

In spite of this doctrine of monotheism, much of religious thought has inadvertently promoted a religion of "dualism" by its misunderstanding of the nature of evil. This misperception holds that Good and Evil are equal and opposing forces—one promoted by God (and a heavenly host of angels) and the other being facilitated by a legion of fallen angels that would sway humankind from its path with temptations of every nature. In the presence of a *One God* understanding, however, this dualistic approach does not adequately address the nature of good and evil.

On one occasion, Cayce scholar Herbert Puryear suggested that, ultimately, there were three ways to deal with the nature of evil: 1) elevate good and evil to primary opposing realities, becoming dualistic in our understanding; 2) deny the existence of evil, suggesting it is only a misperception created by our lower state of awareness; or 3) affirm its reality but assume that it is somehow contained within the ultimate Reality of one God.[18] It is this third approach that is repeatedly confirmed by concepts and ideas in the Edgar Cayce material.

When Morton Blumenthal requested a reading from Cayce in which the "fundamental principles" of both science and religion could be explained, the reading's response not only affirmed monotheism but went on to affirm the "oneness" of all life:

> …The first lesson for *six* months should be *One*—One—One—*One;* Oneness of God, oneness of man's relation, oneness of force, oneness of time, oneness of purpose, *Oneness* in every effort—Oneness—Oneness!   900-429

Although it may be challenging to our third-dimensional understanding, this not only suggests that there is only one God, but it also

---

[18]Herbert B. Puryear, PhD, *The Edgar Cayce Primer* (New York: Bantam Books, 1982), 209-10.

affirms that in all of Creation, *There Is Only God*! In other words, every-thing that exists is a part of God. Everyone and everything is a part of God. There cannot be dualism if the only thing that exists is God. If this is the case and all that exists is a part of God, how can we understand the occurrence of evil?

On many occasions, while discussing the ultimate nature of God, the readings summarize that essence in three simple words: "God is love." Examples include the following: "For, God is love . . . and *is* the Force that permeates all activity." (5749-4) " . . . For truth in any clime is ever the same—it is law. And love is law, law is love. Love is God, God is Love. It is the universal consciousness, the desire for harmonious expressions for the good of all, that is the heritage in man . . . " (3350-1) And "Let the purposes and the desires of thy heart be more and more in accordance with His will. For the Lord thy God is Love . . . " (378-45) This very same premise is contained in scripture in verses such as the following: "He that loveth not knoweth not God; for God is love," (1 John 4:8) and "We have known and believed the love that God hath to us. God is love; and he that dwelleth in love dwelleth in God, and God in him." (1 John 4:16)

So how can we reconcile the Oneness of all Force, the nature of God being essentially Love, and the existence of evil? This same question was in the minds of members of the original Study Group while studying the "Oneness of all force," when they asked, "In relation to the Oneness of all force, explain the popular concept of the Devil . . . " The response came:

> In the beginning, celestial beings. We have first the Son, then the other sons or celestial beings that are given their force and power. Hence that force which rebelled in the unseen forces (or in spirit) that came into activity, was that influence which has been called Satan, the Devil, the Serpent; they are One. That of *rebellion*!
>
> Hence, when man in any activity rebels against the influenc-es of good he harkens to the influence of evil rather than the influence of good . . .
> Evil is rebellion . . .   262-52

A similar response came almost two years later when the group sought an explanation of the phrase contained in John 17:12: "none of them is lost but the son of perdition." Cayce said that the statement was not simply a reference to Judas (who betrayed Jesus) but was instead about anyone who rebels and choses selfishness, materialism, and personal gratification over the things of the spirit:

> Hence that spoken of him that rebelled against the throne of heaven ... chosen rather to seek his *own* ways and to deceive others into seeking to follow their own manner rather than that there should be credence or credit or loyalty or love shown to that source from which life, consciousness or manifestations emanated ....
>
> Then, all are sons of perdition—or allow that force to manifest through them—who deny Him, or who betray Him, or who present themselves to be one thing and—under earthly environment or for personal gain, or for reasons of gratification—do otherwise; for they do but persecute, deny, betray Him.   262-93

The readings indicate that evil is fundamentally rebellion, selfishness, and self-gratification rather than selflessness and acting in accord with spirit and Divine will. It is essentially acting out of accord with spiritual principles and instead giving thought of self in preference to the needs of others; a few examples follow:

> Thus, there is a physical-body and there is a mind-body which the entity may or may not control; may or may not control the appetites of the flesh ... Those who have come to the attitude of seeking physical gratification find that this is plain hell itself. This is very much the attitude of the entity to satisfy it, to gratify it to Satan. This becomes the weakling, the attitude of those who only know gratifying of some physical desire, some appetite, some attribute of the physical body which may be satiated.
>   5250-1

> (Q) What is holding back my spiritual development?
> (A) Nothing holding back—as has just been given—but *self*. For know, as has been given of old, "Though I take the wings of the morning in thought and fly unto the uttermost parts of the

earth, Thou art there! Though I fly into the heavenly hosts, Thou
art there! Though I make my bed in hell, Thou art there!"
      And as He has promised, "When ye cry unto me, *I will hear—*
and answer speedily." Nothing prevents—only self. Keep self
and the shadow away. Turn thy face to the light and the shad-
ows fall behind.   987-4

… for harmony, peace, joy, love, long-suffering, patience, brotherly love, kindness—these are the fruits of the Spirit. Hate, harsh
words, unkind thoughts, oppressions and the like, these are the
fruits of the evil forces, or Satan and the soul either abhors that
it has passed, or enters into the joy of its Lord …   5754-2

Did He not—the Christ, the Maker—say this over and over
again? that so long as spite, selfishness, evil desires, evil communications were manifested, they would give the channels
through which *that* spirit called Satan, devil, Lucifer, Evil One,
might work?   262-119

Since the Cayce information essentially sees evil as selfishness and
the spirit of rebellion manifested, do the readings also indicate that
fallen angels are literal beings? The answer is yes, but the originations
of their existence might be very different than we have supposed. In
fact, there are two distinct possibilities about the nature of fallen angels that seem to be confirmed by the Edgar Cayce readings. The first
possibility is that once souls started to choose things apart from spirit
and godliness, members of the angelic realm agreed to "shepherd" and
be responsible for this rebelliousness in the human creature, thereby
assuring that these souls would eventually return and find their way
back to the Light. The second possibility is that the various hierarchical
rank of angels proposed both Jewish and Catholic tradition as well as
various Church fathers, although not always in the same order (Sera-
phim, Cherubim, Thrones, Dominations, Virtues, Powers, Principalities,
Archangels, and Angels),[19] creates the likelihood that some members

---

[19]*New Catholic Encyclopedia* (Washington, DC: Catholic University of America, 1967), Vol
I: A to AZT, s.v. "Groupings of Angels," 511–13.

of the angelic realms may be in their own process of consciousness development, thereby possessing the ability to make rebellious choices much as their human counterparts. In other words, just as there are human souls who have made choices apart from God, there may be angelic beings who have done the very same thing.

The Cayce readings affirm the idea that fallen angels oversaw aspects of the spirit of rebellion not only so that these souls might become aware of their separation from God but also so that they would eventually be helped to return to the Light because they are "a portion of the Divine." While the original study group explored the lesson of "Destiny," a reading offered the following:

> Man in his former state, or natural state, or permanent consciousness, is soul. Hence in the beginning all were souls of that creation, with the body as of the Creator—of the spirit forces that make manifest in using same in the various phases or experiences of consciousness for the activity.
>
> It has been understood by most of those who have attained to a consciousness of the various presentations of good and evil in manifested forms, as we have indicated, that the prince of this world, Satan, Lucifer, the Devil—as a soul—made those necessities, as it were, of the consciousness in materiality; that man might—or that the soul might—become aware of its separation from the God-force.
>
> Hence the continued warring that is ever present in materiality or in the flesh, or the warring—as is termed—between the flesh and the devil, or the warring between those influences of good and evil.
>
> As the soul is then a portion of the Divine, it must eventually return to that source from which, of which, it is a part ...262-89

In other words, there appear to be some "fallen angels" who took upon the assignment to be separated from the Divine Will as a means of helping humanity; in the language of the readings: " . . . made those necessities, as it were, of the consciousness in materiality; that man might—or that the soul might—become aware of its separation from the God-force." (262-89)

In terms of whether or not there are angels who are in varying degrees of alignment with spirit and their own growth, a reading given to a twenty-one-year-old clerk seems to confirm that just as humans may be separated from God, there are angels and archangels who are "separate from the fullness of the Father":

> Hence, *seek* to know *His* ways with thee. Not alone by denying that sin or error exists. *True*, sin and error is not of God—save through His sons that *brought* error, through selfishness, into the experience of the souls of men, the body by which angels and archangels are separate from the fullness of the Father . . . if there is the manifestation of greed, avarice, hate, selfishnesses, unkindliness, ungodliness, it makes for the harkenings that bring their fruit—contention, strife, hate, avarice, and separation from the light. For, those that have turned their face *from* the light of God can only see shadow or darkness and that light is only for those far away . . .   479-1

On another occasion when Cayce was asked to describe how angels and archangels help humanity, the response suggested that angels exist on various planes of development as a means of helping humanity on those levels grow toward the One Source. These angels may also be involved in a process of consciousness growth that will inevitably enable them to "become one with the first cause [God]":

> . . . With the bringing into creation the manifested forms, there came that which has been, is, and ever will be, the spirit realm and its attributes—designated as angels and archangels. They are the spiritual manifestations in the spirit world of those attributes that the developing forces accredit to the One Source, that may be seen in material planes through the influences that may aid in development of the mental and spiritual forces through an experience—or in the acquiring of knowledge that may aid in the intercourse one with another.
> Then, how do they aid? Under what law do they operate?
> The divine, in its intercourse, influence and manifestation with that which partakes of the same forces as they manifest . . .

> Hence the development is through the planes of experience that an entity may become one *with* the first cause; even as the angels that wait before the Throne bring the access of the influence in the experience through the desires and activities of an entity, or being, in whatever state, place or plane of development the entity is passing.   5749-3

Regardless of whether or not fallen angels are subject to their own path of development or whether they are ultimately responsible for overseeing the rebelliousness of humankind, the readings contend that these influences have absolutely no power over individuals unless they choose to make themselves in accord with this spirit of rebellion. Repeatedly citing Deut. 30:15, "I have set before thee this day life and good, death and evil," individuals were constantly encouraged to make choices in alignment with the universal Christ Consciousness (the awareness of our oneness with God) rather than a selfishness that disregards all others. It is in the process of choosing that we either place ourselves in alignment with a "personal savior" or a "personal devil." (262-52) Obviously, the question is which of these patterns do we wish to emulate and make manifest in our lives? On one occasion that element of choice was expressed, as follows:

> ...For, as of old, it is given to each and every soul, "There is today set before you good and evil, life and death—choose thou." As is the choice, as is known in the experience of each soul, as the application is made in the experience, so are the fruits. "By their fruits ye shall know them."
>
> Then, when a choice has been made that makes for those things that bring contention, avarice, vice, harsh words, know there must be a renewing of self in those hopes and promises He has given. And though the choice has been ill, the activities may bring peace and harmony and understanding, and the glorifying ever to the Father through that it causes the individual to do *to* its neighbor, its friend, its associates. For, as He has given, "He that giveth the cup of cold water in the name of the Son shall in no wise lose his reward," in that harmony, peace and life that is expressed in the activities of such a soul.   505-4

In addition to upholding the mistaken belief that the role of fallen angels is to somehow ensnare human souls, some conservative theology has also repeatedly disseminated information and ideas about a biblical antichrist that may not be accurate. In fact, throughout history this approach has resulted in the discussion of numerous candidates as the possible antichrist that is still being debated on the Internet: various Presidents, Popes, and numerous leaders including the emperor Nero, the emperor Charlemagne, Napoleon, Hitler, Mussolini Stalin, Osama bin Laden, and many others all being identified as likely contenders. This interpretation often suggests that the Book of Revelation is a chronicle of prophetic doom in which the ultimate nemesis of Jesus attempts to take hold of the earth and all who dwell there, leaving mass destruction, chaos, and evil in his wake. This is not the interpretation promoted by the Edgar Cayce readings. In fact, the readings suggest that the entire book is not about external prophecy but is instead about the internal struggle between an individual's higher and lower selves. It was this struggle that the Apostle John described in his visionary experience that came to be called the Book of Revelation, and it is this same struggle that every soul "who seeks to know, to walk in, a closer communion with Him" (281-16) will ultimately encounter:

> For the visions, the experiences, the names, the churches, the places, the dragons, the cities, all are but emblems of those forces that may war within the individual in its journey through the material, or from the entering into the material manifestation to the entering into the glory, or the awakening in the spirit ...
>
> 218-16

Ultimately, just what does the Bible say about the antichrist? Many individuals might be surprised to learn that the word "antichrist" does not even appear in the Book of Revelation. The word appears only in the epistles of John and suggests that an antichrist is any individual who denies the identity of Jesus as the Christ (see especially 1 John 2:22 and 1 John 4:3). In other words, rather than being some kind of a worldwide archenemy, it is simply the act of not believing that Jesus is the Christ.

Cayce's approach to studying the Book of Revelation came as a re-

sult of numerous readings that suggested a connection could be found
between the endocrine centers of the body, an individual's growth in
awareness, anatomy, and the symbolism of the Revelation. For example,
in January 1930, a twenty–year–old woman was checked into the Edgar
Cayce Hospital after having been treated for ten years by other physi-
cians for "nervous irritability." Her symptoms included: uncontrollable
twitching of the face, hands, and limbs; an irritable disposition, and the
inability to control her volatile emotions even in public. During one of
the girl's health readings, Cayce suggested that it would be beneficial
for the doctor in charge of the case to read the Book of Revelation
and to try and understand the Revelation especially in relationship to
what was occurring within the body and mind of the young woman.
Similar advice was given to a forty–one–year–old housewife who was
told that she should compare and contrast the Book of Revelation with
Gray's Anatomy (264–15). During a follow–up reading, the woman was
informed that the Book of Revelation provided an understanding of
what transpired within an individual " . . . when the vibrations are
raised within the body through meditation, or through that of fasting
and prayer . . . " (264–19)

On another occasion, Cayce advised a middle–aged chiropractor that
if he really wanted to understand himself and others, he needed to read
the Book of Revelation "with the idea of the body as the interpretation."
The reading went on to discuss the importance of choice and either following the rebellious spirit or the pattern demonstrated by the Christ:

> So, as in the self, whether the individual entity or soul entertains
> its relationship to the Creative Forces or not, the relationship is
> still existent or possible. For indeed in Him, the Father-God, ye
> move and have thy being. Act like it! Don't act like ye think ye are
> a God! Ye may become such, but when ye do ye think not of thy-
> self. For what is the pattern? He thought it not robbery to make
> Himself equal with God, but He acted like it in the earth. He
> made Himself of no estate that you, through His grace, through
> His mercy, through His sacrifice might have an advocate with
> that First Cause, God; that first principle, spirit.
>
> What are you doing about it? In thine own self ye will find
> that it is thine self. Selfishness is the basic sin . . . ye may apply the

principles of truth, patience, longsuffering, brotherly love, kindness, gentleness. For if ye would be forgiven, ye must forgive.
These are unchangeable laws. Thy body, thyself is the temple of
the living God. That is all the God ye may know, that which ye
apply in thy relationship to thy fellow man. For the manner in
which ye (as an individual entity, a body, a mind, a soul) treat thy
fellow man is the manner in which ye treat thy Maker. Remember that what ye sow, thine own soul, thine own entity, thine
own mind, thine own body must reap. Ye are already in eternity,
thy soul has been since the beginning. What are ye doing about
it? ...   4083-1

In addition to these readings and others, over a period of ten years
(1933–1943) members of a prayer group calling themselves the "Glad
Helpers" obtained readings on interpreting the Book of Revelation.
Originally founded in 1931, the prayer group consisted of individuals
interested in prayer, meditation, and spiritual healing. The rationale
for studying the Revelation was that it would better enable them to
understand the points of contact between the spirit and the physical
structures of the body. Cayce told the group that the Apostle John had
sought prayer and meditation in order to understand his work after the
death of Jesus. The experience that resulted was a vision of the internal
struggle that takes place in each individual between the higher and
lower selves as consciousness growth and soul development takes place.

Aside from the word antichrist, the Revelation does contain numerous images of dangerous beasts, dragons, and malevolent creatures that
would seem to be set on creating destruction upon the earth. What
do the readings suggest about these images? Rather than interpreting
every symbol in the Revelation, an exploration of a few of them may
be sufficient to confirm the information obtained by the Glad Helpers
Prayer Group.[20]

The body contains seven endocrine centers that the readings indicate
have a vibrational and spiritual connection with the soul. Those seven
centers consist of four lower centers (gonads, cells of Leydig, adrenals,

---

[20]For a more detailed examination of Cayce's interpretation of the Book of Revelation, see: Kevin J. Todeschi, *Edgar Cayce on Soul Symbolism* (Virginia Beach, VA: Yazdan
Publishing, 2003).

and thymus) and three higher centers (thyroid, pineal, and pituitary). With this in mind, the repeated references to "seven" in the Book of Revelation all correspond to activities at the level of each of these centers (e.g. seven churches, seven golden candlesticks, seven plagues, seven angels with seven vials, seven trumpets with seven angels, seven stars, etc.). It may be important to point out that rather than thinking the lower self is somehow evil or bad, the lower self is simply something each individual encounters in the process of personal growth. The issue is not whether there is a lower self but instead how long we allow it to hold dominion over our true spiritual nature.

As John meditated, the energy of the kundalini apparently rose through his endocrine centers, and it was the movement of that energy which evoked images of the first four beasts, corresponding to each of the first four centers that had been awakened in meditation: the calf = the gonads; the man = the cells of Leydig; the lion = the adrenals; and the eagle = the thymus. This interpretation is especially interesting when you compare the images to virtually the very same experience had by the prophet Ezekiel 500 years earlier when he had "visions" of four creatures that each possessed four faces: "the face of a man," "the face of a lion," "the face of an ox," and "the face of an eagle." (Ezek. 1:10). In terms of how each of these images relates to the lower self, Cayce correlated them with the four basic natures of personal survival: self-sustenance (gonads), self-propagation (cells of Leydig), self-preservation (adrenals), and self–gratification (thymus).

The prayer group eventually realized that there was also a symbolic connection between the four elements and the four lower spiritual centers, as follows: air = thymus; fire = adrenals; water = cells of Leydig; and earth = gonads. As these lower centers become purified through the activity of the higher self, the resulting imagery uses the elements of the earth to portray such things as hail, fire, and flood coming as devastations upon the earth. Edgar Cayce reminded the prayer group that all of the destructive passages were not about external events but were rather associated with influences within self that were at war with one another until the process of purification had taken place: " . . . Do not confuse the interpretation with that outside of thyself . . . " (281–30) With that in mind, when the Revelation imagery portrays portions of the earth being destroyed, it corresponds to those portions of the body that remain rebellious or are out of alignment becoming transformed. When the imagery portrays much of humankind being killed or destroyed, it corresponds to individual cells that are out of attunement being purified, eliminated, or transformed, as well.

The most fearsome of the beasts portrayed in the Revelation imagery may well be the two beasts in Revelation 13.

> And I stood upon the sand of the sea, and saw a beast rise up out of the sea, having seven heads and ten horns, and upon his horns ten crowns, and upon his heads the name of blasphemy.
>
> And the beast which I saw was like unto a leopard, and his feet were as the feet of a bear, and his mouth as the mouth of a lion: and the dragon gave him his power, and his seat, and great authority.   Rev. 13:1-2

> And I beheld another beast coming up out of the earth; and he had two horns like a lamb, and he spake as a dragon . . .
>
> And he causeth all, both small and great, rich and poor, free and bond, to receive a mark in their right hand, or in their foreheads:
>
> And that no man might buy or sell, save he that had the mark, or the name of the beast, or the number of his name.
>
> Here is wisdom. Let him that hath understanding count the number of the beast: for it is the number of a man; and his number is Six hundred threescore and six.
>   Rev. 13: 11, 16-18

The symbolism of the beast possessing seven heads and ten horns (Rev. 13:1) is similar to the dragon in Revelation 12:3 with seven heads and ten horns. In both cases the seven heads are associated with the rebellious nature of each of the seven spiritual centers, and the ten horns correspond to the conflicting desires within each of the five senses that war with one another. Chapter 12 also details the "war in heaven" between the archangel Michael and the red dragon, which is symbolic of the conflict between one's spiritual higher self and one's selfish lower nature. Cayce told the prayer group that this conflict was illustrated " . . . by the war between the Lord of the Way and the Lord of Darkness—or the Lord of Rebellion." (281-33)

In terms of the second beast that is associated with the number "six hundred three score and six" (666), thoughts on this beast have given rise to fearful prognostications throughout much of religious history because the text suggests that no one will be able to "buy or sell, save he that had the mark ..." (Rev. 13:17) The Cayce readings suggest that putting self in accord with the mark of the beast is simply indicative of putting self's will and desires above the will of God. Another way of considering this might be to remember that since there are seven spiritual centers—the seventh of which is associated with the soul's awareness of its oneness with God—anything less than seven (e.g. six) could be an indication of someone that lacks the "consciousness of God." (281-34)

Perhaps more than anything else, personal rebelliousness defines any individual or activity that falls short of God Consciousness. The readings, however, would suggest that the attainment of that consciousness is our collective destiny. It is simply a matter of time. When the Glad Helpers Prayer Group asked about the meaning of Revelation 20:1-3 in which an angel comes down from haven and bounds Satan for a thousand years, Cayce provided encouraging news: there will come a time in the history of the world when enough individuals are so committed to manifesting spiritual principles in the earth that the rebellious spirit will be contained. At that time only those souls who have chosen to manifest the oneness of God will be able to incarnate, making it possible for them to reach God consciousness. The reading encouraged the group, "Be *ye all determined* within thy minds, thy hearts, thy purposes, to be of that number!" (281-37)

The Edgar Cayce material provides a unique approach to the topic of fallen angels, the antichrist, and the lower self. In summary, the readings repeatedly confirm that the evolution of consciousness has been integrally woven with the unfolding universe ever since God moved all of Creation into being. Some fallen angels may be on their own path toward growth and development; others may be guardians of those souls who make choices outside the parameters of Divine will. The antichrist is not some global nemesis who threatens spirit and the human condition but is instead a mistaken awareness that denies the reality of God Consciousness being made manifest in the earth. Cayce however confirms that this not only transpired in the life of Jesus but also resides as a potential within each and every soul. It is the struggle between one's god-self and one's human-self that is depicted in the Apostle John's Revelation that each of us encounters in our own movement through space and time.

7

Contemporary Encounters with Angels

Both scripture and the Edgar Cayce readings confirm that individuals experience angelic encounters. From the perspective of Cayce and the Bible, a number of these encounters are never recognized as such because of humankind's propensity to remain "unaware," but there are individuals throughout history who remain convinced that they have personally experienced an interaction of some kind with a spiritual being that was not human. For those who are aware of experiencing such encounters, there is often the feeling that they occurred at just the right time: people who were in the midst of sorrow or self-pity found joy and relief; those who felt confused and abandoned often found direction; and those who were worried or afraid found comfort and relief. Repeatedly, individuals who have had a contemporary encounter with a divine being explain how it provided guidance, intercession, encouragement, and even a sense of hope and unconditional love.

In the case of Tilly Alfonsi, an angelic encounter not only transformed her but also gave her reassurance that angels had been a part of her life even during the most challenging times of her childhood. Now a spiritual healer, an enthusiast of the Rudolf Steiner material, and on the board of an educational foundation, she left her role as editor–in–chief of a successful woman's magazine in her forties to pursue the spiritual because of her angelic encounter. In describing her life, Tilly states that for years she felt lonely and isolated. In her words, "I was a lonely and abused child who continued to feel as lonely and abused as an adult."

One evening, Tilly was alone, lost in thought, and walking in a neighborhood park under the brilliance of the moon. All at once a beautiful angel with magnificent wings appeared to her and began to smile:

> I was completely breathless. She told me she was an angel of purity and her name was Shushianae. She told me she had been with me all the time. I suddenly realized that the imaginary friends I had had as a child had been angels. I felt my heart beating. I felt blessed. She told me she had always been next to me, but I had been too busy to see or feel her. She told me I needed to pray.

The angel told her that she had often interacted with Tilly in her dreams. She reassured her that all was well and that she was loved. Just as suddenly as Shushianae had appeared, suddenly the angel was gone.

Although brief in duration, Tilly's experience left a lasting imprint upon her. She admits that from that time forward, she has never felt lonely again. She began a spiritual search and changed her life completely. She began to work with prayer, and now prays constantly. She developed a close relationship with Jesus. She began working with spiritual healing and the goal of helping individuals become whole themselves: "I want to help people know that they can enjoy life, be happy, and heal as many issues as possible." She describes her life as being one of bliss and service and filled with an understanding that "the only thing that matters is love." When asked about her understanding of the role of Shushianae in her life in the present, Tilly smiles and says simply, "She is still next to me all the time."

Linda James has no doubt that on at least two different occasions she has seen some kind of an energetic being that was either an angelic presence or a spirit guide. The first occasion happened nearly thirty

years ago at a time when she was having intense challenges with a relationship. In love with a married man, she became depressed, stopped
eating and sleeping, and eventually sought psychiatric help. She also
collected books that helped her through that challenging time.

One day, she remembers walking along North Avenue Beach in Chicago, carrying the book *The Tao of Pooh* by Benjamin Hoff. The volume
explores Eastern philosophy using the characters from the Winnie the
Pooh story and essentially presents the premise that it is possible to
stay centered and calm no matter what is occurring in your life. Although long interested in God, for Linda the book was a part of her
transformational process.

No one else seemed to be around as she continued her walk. Suddenly, a stocky, balding man with a ring of white hair came upon her
and asked, "Is that book like *The Lost Continent of Mu?*" Linda replied that
she didn't know and continued walking. A moment later she turned
around, but there was no one there. She was alone on North Avenue
Beach. Somehow, he had just disappeared! She remembered the book
title and eventually found it. That book helped lead her to a broader
understanding of life and the exploration of such things as ancient mysteries, reincarnation, the Edgar Cayce material, and like-minded people.

The second time Linda had the experience was when she was
walking her dog near their Chicago home. What she describes as an
"energetic being" was about twenty feet in front of her and crossed her
path. Her first thought was that it might be some kind of an extrater-
restrial because it seemed to be glowing with a white-light energy. Her
dog could see it as well because he started barking, but whatever it
was did not turn to acknowledge her or the barking dog. No one else
was around, and just as quickly as she had seen the individual, it was
gone. Linda has no doubt that both experiences occurred; both have
simply been absorbed into her understanding that we are not alone
and that we are all participants in an ongoing process to manifest our
full potential.

Although she has never seen an angel, Betty Adams is absolutely
convinced that her life was saved on two different occasions due to
intervention from the angelic realms. Both experiences happened in
her car. In the first, she had just stopped at the same gas station she
always uses near a busy intersection. Because of the location of the

station near the traffic signal, whenever the light is red, cars block the exit from the station onto the main road. Usually, Betty positions her car just out of the exit onto the highway's shoulder "until some nice person lets me cut into the traffic." However, on this occasion after she had filled her tank and was getting ready to position her car as she always did, she distinctly heard a voice exclaim: "It is not a good idea." Without questioning the voice, Betty stopped the car far short of where she usually maneuvered. All at once, a large red pickup truck came speeding down along the shoulder of the highway, so close to Betty's car that her automobile literally shook with a rush of wind as the truck sped by. She suddenly realized that had she been positioned where she usually was, the truck would have hit her at high speed, directly impacting the driver's door—there was no doubt that she would have been killed instantly.

The second experience occurred when Betty was driving home from the grocery store after getting supplies for a Halloween party. The weather was cold and it had started to rain. As she was driving, she was suddenly hit with the feeling that she had to drive faster. She pushed her foot on the gas and sped as quickly as she could. Suddenly, there was a loud "crack" as though a rock had broken through the window just behind her head. When she got home, it became clear that she had not heard a rock; instead, a bullet had actually entered the window just behind her head and had exited the rear window also breaking the curved glass at the rear of her hatchback.

The next day, the news reported that three blonde woman driving similar cars had all been shot at on the same stretch of road that night. No one had been injured, but one of the other women had been threatened earlier that day at her job in a car impound yard. Drug dealers had demanded that she release their car, and when she didn't, they threatened to kill her. Betty was convinced that "once again, an otherworldly force kept me from getting killed."

Carol Jenkins and her husband talked about divorce for a number of years before actually following through on it. Part of the delay was that they had raised three children. They had also been together since they were about twenty years old, and with each delay their time together grew until twenty years had passed. During one of the challenging times, Carol had initiated divorce, and, although unhappy, her husband was not ready to commit to separating. Oftentimes, Carol found herself angry, and her husband remained distant. Obviously, they were unhappy as a couple, but they were somehow frozen in their dysfunction. One night they were both lying in bed, nearly falling asleep, when something entered the room, According to Carol:

> We were almost asleep when a brilliant white light Presence appeared on my side of the bed. I was startled and realized that the Presence was on his side of the bed too! We were virtually frozen and unable to move a muscle. We were both in awe. The light suddenly subsided and then was gone. My husband whispered, "What was that?" Still unable to move, all I could say was: "I don't know!"

Although she doesn't know why the experience happened to them, it obviously came at a time when they both needed assistance and comfort. For Carol, it would become one in a series of experiences that gave her reassurance that God is real and available whenever He is needed.

The intervention of an angelic presence also seemed to be the case in the life of Barbara Jackson after she called out for help. She and her husband, Mike, were motorcycle buffs who traveled extensively. The couple had lost their son when he was only twenty-three and riding somehow gave them personal relief from his death as well as the opportunity to be together.

To Barbara's horror, Mike was diagnosed with a progressive illness within a year after their son's death. It got to the point that Mike could no longer help balance their motorcycle, as they owned a large 1500 Honda Goldwing. In order to continue their outings together, they had it converted to a three-wheeled trike. That had been a blessing to them as, according to Barbara, "Since Mike could no longer hold up the bike, it allowed me to drive and take him all around as his illness progressed." The following year, Mike passed away and Barbara wanted the motorcycle to be a part of his funeral: "We took my husband on the back of that trike in a small box from the funeral at the church to the cemetery to inter his ashes."

Losing both a son and a husband within two years was a devastating experience. Barbara had already lost her trust in God after losing her son, and just when she was working on getting it back, her husband was gone. Obviously, there were plenty of challenges, especially when loneliness creeped in. For the next two years, Barbara did her best to maintain her sanity by continuing to work, spending time with her other two grown children and riding the trike. Still, she was often lonely and depressed.

One day she was out riding the trike when black clouds filled the horizon, and it became apparent that an enormous storm was imminent. Barbara worried that she needed to find shelter immediately, as she was from a part of the country known for large pieces of hail, which could turn deadly in a storm. All at once, her situation became even worse:

> I was on the busiest street in town, trying to hurry to any place I could get to find shelter when the bike stalled and I couldn't get it started again and in gear. I tried over and over again and began to panic as rain and small hail started falling. I started to cry. I prayed, "Please, God, help me!"
>
> Just at that moment, someone walked up behind me and helped me get the motorcycle started and in gear again. The bike started and I drove away and turned to wave and thank the person who had helped me. There was no one there.

Barbara made it to an over entrance for a hotel, just as enormous pieces of hail started to fall. She has no doubt that divine intervention had been sent her way: "I thanked God over and over again for saving me." The experience reawakened her belief in God. It helped her get through the challenging days and encouraged her to continue her spiritual journey. When asked what she has learned since the experience, Barbara is quick to respond: "I no longer fear death; I know God is love. I trust all is as it should be."

Alexis Davies spent years overcoming all of the emotional damage done by her family and those around her while she was growing up. She always felt different, but it wasn't really until her husband introduced her to the philosophy of New Thought that life started to make sense to her. It was a way of thinking that enabled her to overcome some of the challenges of her past. And it instilled in her the fact that she wanted to raise her own children in a very different environment. When her first son was about seven, he was on his bike and Alexis was following close behind when an angelic encountered came totally unexpectedly:

> My son was riding his bike ahead of me while I walked. It was sunny and warm. We had just turned the corner on the sidewalk when I suddenly saw an image of a male figure walking directly ahead of us. He was walking about a foot *above* the ground. He was wearing leather sandals, and wore robes which flowed with his movement.
>
> I somehow knew that it was my Guardian Angel, and I was stunned! Although ahead, his speed matched our pace. I felt an overwhelming sense of being protected, and then he was gone. It was a confirmation that all was well, and that I was on the right track.

An unexpected angel appeared to Evelyn Martin when she took her friend to the hospital for a surgical procedure. The surgery was scheduled for the first thing in the morning, and they had arrived at the hospital before daybreak. Her friend was understandably nervous, and as they drove into the parking lot, she asked Evelyn if the two of them could pray together before going into the building. Evelyn agreed, parked the car in the almost deserted lot, and began to pray with her friend for a positive outcome to the surgery. As Evelyn describes it:

> I suddenly saw an enormous glowing figure standing over the middle of the surgical center. It was enormous, like a Macy's Thanksgiving Day balloon. It seemed like a male energy, very powerful and protective. I was so surprised by what I could see that I began to tremble.
>
> I began to describe what I was seeing to my friend. She told me that she was covered with goosebumps and chills as I described it.
>
> Suddenly, the angelic figure moved towards us. It came to the same corner of the parking lot where we were sitting. All at once, it knelt down on the right side of the car and began to pray with us!

The experience lasted for only a few moments and then was over. Evelyn and her friend walked into the hospital, and the surgery turned out just fine. It was an incredible experience that has stayed with her ever since. In thinking back upon the encounter, Evelyn adds finally: "I wish I could see it again."

Another example of a visitation by an angel is told by Doug Gaines. In order to understand the impact that the story had on him, Doug provides the following: "At the time of my encounter experience, I was a slave to alcoholism. Today, I am married and the father of one child. When I was younger, I had a relationship with a young woman with whom I was very much in love."

Long interested in spirituality, in his forties Doug decided that an avenue of service that appealed to him was helping dying veterans who were in hospice. That motivation led him to a three–day training course put on by the Veterans Administration hospitals. The program's purpose was to walk volunteers through the many potential scenarios that can occur during the death process. One of the exercises was a guided meditation in which participants were taken through a reverie and asked to visit a "happy place." When Doug heard "happy place," he began to visualize one of his favorite places in the world: the beach at Stone Harbor, New Jersey. To his surprise, however, he was suddenly transported somewhere else, where he encountered an angel:

> I was immediately teleported to a beach on the Hatteras Island National Seashore, on the Outer Banks of North Carolina.
>
> Suddenly, I was standing alone on the beach facing the Atlantic Ocean. The cloud ceiling overhead was low enough that throwing a ball into the air might reach it. Then out of the clouds, maybe twenty-five meters in front of me, an angel began to materialize!
>
> During the materialization, I noticed that the particles had a digital characteristic to them, with my closest approximation being that it looked like the construction of CGI animation. Once in complete form, the angel floated down to stand on the beach in front of me.
>
> He appeared to have freckles and a receding hairline and displayed a compassionate, yet knowing smirk. He emitted a

cobalt blue energy. He moved closer until I was engulfed in the cloak of his blue embrace—it was like being in a dome of comforting blue light. I put my head on his shoulder and began to lose consciousness.

He repeated his name five times; at the same moment I could hear the voice of the group regressionist bringing us back to consciousness. I cannot overstate how truly vivid the experience was.

When Doug was back in the room with other hospice volunteers, he wondered why he had gone to Hatteras instead of New Jersey, and then it hit him. It was at Hatteras that he had been with his first love, and there—unbeknownst to him at the time—they had conceived a child. It was only later, months after they had broken up, that the young woman had told him she had obtained an abortion; it had caused Doug a great deal of sadness and personal conflict.

When asked how the angelic encounter has impacted him, Doug asserts without hesitation: "My angelic visitation served as a major signpost on my pilgrimage to redemption." The experience prompted a healing on many levels. In terms of the aborted child and his previous relationship, Doug admits: "I have mourned and cried and asked for forgiveness for my role." But he has come to understand some of the karmic connections with his previous relationship and does not regret the time they spent together. After the visitation he also went to a therapist and, after only one session, broke his connection to alcohol. He remains interested in service—serving others as well as his family. Since the experience, he has also become much more compassionate and humble. He remains forever grateful for the encounter which led to, what he calls, "a charmed life." Doug adds, "I remain a very happy non-drinker. It is no exaggeration to state that my sobriety is much preferred to the slavery of alcoholism—that has been my greatest life lesson of all."

Ruth Jenkins tells the story of having tremendous pain and increasing discomfort in her legs and knees. Only in her early seventies, the pain was making it difficult to walk. It had gotten to the point of being a daily struggle, as the pain was debilitating. She thought she was having problems with progressive arthritis. When it was diagnosed as something else, she admits that she was somehow encouraged: "When I discovered it was Lyme disease, I was so relieved that it wasn't arthritis!"

Along with seeing regular doctors, when Ruth got the Lyme diagnosis she began to work with homeopathic remedies. She also admits that one of the things she likes to do while driving is to sing. She has a massage practice, which she continued in spite of her leg pains, and she often sings on her way to work. Ruth describes what happened on one occasion while she was singing in the car:

> I was making up songs in praise of God while I was driving to where I practice massage each Thursday. I was singing as I often do when all of a sudden, I heard the sounds of other voices singing with me. I became aware of beautiful voices all around me. They were deep and warm and sounded like they were coming from far away.
>
> And then I realized they were singing the songs I was singing as I was making the song up. The first thought that came to me was, "How do they know the words to my songs?" and the second thought was, "Angels!"

Later that day when Ruth arrived home, she noticed that her legs felt different. Her legs felt much better. Somehow after the experience, Ruth's Lyme disease was gone! Eventually, the doctor confirmed that there was no evidence of Lyme disease. It was truly gone.

Today, Ruth is still taking physical therapy to regain the debilitation in her legs caused by the disease, but she is improving. She no longer has the horrendous pain. She has come to see the experience in a spiritual light, and she remains grateful for the miracle of healing that somehow arrived on angel song.

Dorothea Stevens has experienced a number of life's challenges but has always found the faith and perseverance to continue. After just seven years of marriage, her husband committed suicide, making her a single parent to their daughter and a widow at the age of thirty-one. In time, she would return to college, earn her master's degree in social welfare, and study the role of music therapy in death and dying. Her angelic encounter occurred when she was in her fifties.

Always interested in things of the spirit, she has sought meaning in many different directions. On one occasion, she was drawn to a class at a New Thought Church, which promised the opportunity to get in touch with your angel. After getting quiet and saying a prayer of protection, Dorothea describes what happened next:

> We were instructed to quiet our minds and open ourselves to an angelic presence. I remember feeling my usual doubt that I would feel anything and I'd be embarrassed to admit it when other participants shared their experiences afterward. To my surprise, when I asked for a name in my mind, the response came back: "Robert." I immediately thought, "What kind of an angel's name is that? Robert?!" A little later, I made the connection.
>
> Several years before I was born, my mother had given birth to a son with spina bifida. There was no cure at the time for an open spine, only providing around-the-clock comfort and changing of dressing for as long as the child lived. She had named him Bobby, and he lived just under a year.
>
> Although I never knew him, over the years my Mother frequently and often tearfully shared her loving remembrances of Bobby. She said that when he looked into her eyes, it was though he was telling her that he knew she was doing everything she could for him. There was a very strong soul connection between Mother and Bobby.
>
> I knew in my soul that Robert was Bobby.

About six weeks later, Dorothea got a call from her sister that their eighty–nine–year–old mother had fallen and was in the hospital awaiting surgery for a broken hip. The older woman had lost her enthusiasm for living. Dorothea's father had been dead for three years, and Dorothea was convinced that her mother was going to use the broken hip as her end of the road; she would not make it out of surgery. Knowing there was no time to drive to the hospital before the surgery took place, Dorothea got quiet in her sunroom and imagined her mother lying in the hospital room.

> There was no time for me to drive the 200 miles to say goodbye.

I decided to say my goodbyes to her in my imagination. As I saw her lying in her hospital bed, I told her I supported her making the choice to cross over. All at once I felt the same presence that had identified itself as Robert. He let me know that he was in the room with my mother and would help her cross over. He also gave me comfort over the fact that I was not going to be able to be with her during her final hours.

I couldn't write it off as my imagination, I knew that this brother whom I had never met in life and with whom I had never communicated with the exception of those two experiences was indeed an angel who was there to offer safe passage to our mother and spiritual comfort to me!

In terms of what the experience has taught, Dorothea admits that she has no fear of death, and she repeats the words of a song that she often sings to dying patients as a hospice volunteer: "In the end what matters most is how well did we live, how well did we love, and how well did we learn to let go."

It was a beautiful October day in the warm comforting sun of southern Florida when Alice and David Dawson joined seven of their friends in a motor-home vacation from Ft. Lauderdale on the Atlantic Coast to Ft. Myers on the Gulf side with plans to spend a few days along the coast. The motor home belonged to Albert and Juanita. Albert drove and David acted as co-pilot as the remaining seven lounged on sofas and chairs in the back of the motor home. The group was filled with laughter and conversation as they journeyed joyfully along Alligator Alley—the highway connecting the east and west coasts of the peninsula. For some reason, Alice was moved to pray for the group that they would have a safe and enjoyable vacation. As she remembers it, "I prayed for a legion of angels and asked that the white light surround all of us and the motor home."

A few minutes after she had prayed, a car started honking next to them. Albert looked out his side window and saw another driver trying to get their attention. The driver pointed toward the motor home engine. Immediately, Albert could see what the driver was pointing at: smoke was coming from his engine! As soon as Albert pulled off to the side of the highway, the engine immediately burst into flames. The motor home came to an abrupt halt, and everyone evacuated within moments.

All nine of the passengers were able to escape just as the fire consumed the entire engine area and then began spreading to the rest of the motor home. Albert called 911 with his cell phone, but the fire was so quick that by the time the fire trucks arrived, the motor home and all of its contents were completely destroyed. Only the passengers had survived. Bystanders, firemen, policeman, paramedics, and even the local television news stopped to help. Thankfully none of the travelers were injured. Except for losing their luggage and having their vacation cut short, everyone was fine.

When they were heading home, David pulled their car over at a convenience store and let Alice go in to make a purchase. According to Alice:

> A beautiful young girl was working at the store. She and I were the only ones there. As I made my purchase, she looked at me for no reason and said, "Please be safe. Drive carefully and be safe, please," saying it at least five times. I thought it very strange that someone so young would be so concerned, especially since she knew nothing about me or the experience we had just encountered.
>
> I looked back at her as I walked out of the store and as I saw her walking away from me, I had a strange feeling and wondered: "Was I in the presence of an angel?"

Three nights later, Alice had a dream about her deceased father. He appeared to her in the dream and had the most beautiful look on his face. His eyes were filled with love. Alice looked at him and told him how much she missed and loved him: "He didn't speak to me but just kept looking at her with his beautiful smile." All at once, Alice noticed that he was wearing a fireman's hat! She awoke convinced that he had also been one of the angels who had helped them safely through the fire.

In the case of Bess Thomas, she was in her early twenties and in a very abusive relationship when an angelic encounter occurred and became part of the impetus for her to change her life. She had fallen in love and moved in with a young man, and although it had seemed like a good relationship in the very beginning, things soon turned for the worst.

Unbeknownst to Bess at the time, he was abusive, extremely jealous, and addicted to drugs. It wasn't too long until her experience became one in which "he would go into jealous rages, beat me up, and keep me from leaving the house." She had a good job and often had to wear makeup to cover the bruises on her face and body. On occasion, he threatened to kill her. This went on for three years. The final straw came when he hit her so hard while she was sleeping that he broke her jaw.

> I was sitting alone in my apartment, extremely depressed and crying alone. It was early in the morning. Suddenly, out of the corner of my eye, I saw a *huge*, tall, white creature with wings. He tapped my right shoulder. I couldn't believe what I was seeing! My mind wanted to tell me it was not possible!
>
> I *knew* this was an angel, and he was trying to comfort me. Yes, it did comfort me. I did not get any verbal communication but I felt peace.

After the experience, Bess started a spiritual journey. She started to become more self-aware. She started seeing a great therapist. She started thinking about herself. She started meditating and doing breathwork. She started to heal and get on with her life. Looking back on the experience, Bess states: "Sometimes my mind tells me to doubt it, but I know I saw and was touched by an angel. It is something I will never forget."

It was during a period of loneliness and self-pity that Fran McArthur says her own angelic encounter took place. After having experienced an extremely challenging year because of work issues, relationship issues, and personal issues, Fran decided that she just had to get out of town. She had a friend who lived in Italy, and so the two made plans for her to leave the United States and fly to Rome for Christmas. She would arrive by Christmas afternoon, have Christmas dinner with her friend and her friend's family, and then spend a few days at their seaside home. It all sounded like a welcome relief from all of her life's challenges.

Unfortunately for Fran, as soon as she had arrived in Italy, she tele-

phoned her friend and discovered that the entire family had suddenly
fallen ill with the flu and all her Christmas plans had been cancelled.
Her friend reassured her that in a couple of days she would probably
be well enough, and they could spend some time together, but Fran
was devastated. It was just one more disappointment in a year of challenges. Fran checked into a hotel, and although she was in Rome, she
was totally by herself: "the next two days were some of the loneliest I
had ever spent . . . holidays are for families, and I seemed to be the only
person in the entire city who was alone." Finally, the two days passed,
and her friend called to say that she was still sick but could manage to
meet for a short visit and a cup of coffee. According to Fran:

> As I hung up the phone, I was overcome by feelings of self-pity. I
> felt stupid for spending so much money on a trip that was turn-
> ing into a disaster. The problems I'd been facing all year came
> flooding back to me, and I felt lonely and unwanted. As I looked
> into the mirror, I saw only an aging, unhappy woman. The night
> before I'd read a meditation on how we're all here on earth to
> help each other, but it was of no comfort to me. My self-pity was
> so great that I was convinced I didn't have anyone in the world
> who would care to help me, even if I deserved it.

Since her friend lived in the suburbs, Fran had to take the subway
to meet her. She easily found the subway, but once she got there, she
didn't know how to purchase the ticket from the machine as her Italian
was not good enough to understand the instructions. Because it was
the Christmas holiday, there was no one else around to ask. Having no
choice, she dropped several coins into the slot, but nothing happened.
She inserted more coins, and still nothing. Her unhappiness and pity
began to grow. Suddenly, she heard a voice next to her ask in perfect
English, "Is there something I can do to help you?" According to Fran:

> I turned to see a young man, probably early thirties, medium
> height, blond curly hair, very blue eyes, and a sweet face. He
> looked into my eyes with an earnest expression and said, "Please
> don't be afraid. I only want to help you. These machines can be
> very confusing."

Fran assured him that she would be very grateful for his help. He put some more coins in the machine, pushed a couple of buttons, and out popped a ticket. He then showed her how she had to take the ticket to have it stamped by a second machine for validation—something Fran admits she would never have figured out on her own. He handed Fran the ticket and asked where she was headed. She told him that she was going to the Ponte Lungo stop, and he said he was going in the same direction and would accompany her. Once again, he told her, "Don't be afraid. I mean you no harm." She told him she wasn't afraid and would be grateful for the company. He said his name was Adrian. Fran describes the rest of their time together, as follows:

The train arrived and we sat down next to each other. We chatted some more. I told him how much I appreciated his help and he replied, "Don't you know? That's why we're all here, to help one another." His words, though not particularly profound, stunned me. They were exactly what I'd been thinking not two hours before at the hotel. I suddenly couldn't think of anything to say and just stared at the floor for the rest of the journey. When the train came to the stop, we left the train and headed for the escalator.

Then Adrian asked, "May I tell you something?" I glanced at him sideways and his expression was again earnest. He said, "You are a very beautiful woman." Again, I was stunned and speechless. He repeated, "Please don't be afraid. I am not here to harm you. I just need to tell you that you are a beautiful woman." Actually, I was not at all afraid. There was nothing creepy or predatory about him. Nevertheless, I was a bit overwhelmed and didn't know what to make of him. In the subway station was a bar where I was meeting my friend. She hadn't arrived yet, so I asked if he wanted a coffee. He said that he needed to go and we shook hands. For a moment, time stood still. His hand was very, very hot, as though he had a dangerously high fever, but he looked the picture of health. The moment passed. We said goodbye and he turned and left.

As he walked away, I felt completely disoriented. Then it occurred to me that what had made this encounter especially unusual was that, throughout it all, Adrian had been entirely focused on me. From hello to goodbye, he didn't pay attention to other people or look around at his surroundings. It was not something I had ever experienced before.

Several weeks later, Fran was back home and was visiting a close friend who was very psychic. She had not told anyone of her encounter with Adrian. Suddenly, her friend looked up at her and apropos of nothing exclaimed, "Oh, you didn't tell me you met an angel when you were in Rome!" The statement seemed a clear reminder of the biblical statement, "Be not forgetful to entertain strangers: for thereby some have entertained angels unawares." (Heb. 13:2)

Years later, as Fran looks back on her experience she says that she understands the meaning of her encounter with Adrian. Tears still come to her eyes even now; as she thinks about it, "He brought me a message from God reminding me how much He loved me and how much He wanted a closer relationship with me . . . I was filled with a gratitude and humility that I'd never experienced before."

In many different ways, the contemporary experiences of individuals who have angelic encounters affirm the ongoing presence of spirit that remains very much concerned and involved in the affair of humankind. Sometimes the divine presence comes as an affirmation, reassuring those who need it most that they are loved and protected. Sometimes it comes when guidance is needed and there appears no where else to turn. Most often, individuals who have had a divine encounter remain steadfast in their conviction that the experience confirmed that they are loved and that the divine remains very much aware of what is occurring in their lives. Perhaps more than anything else the presence of angels and guides and other emissaries of the Creator all confirm that we are much more than a physical body and that we are never really alone.

Conclusion

In hundreds of readings given over a forty-year period, Edgar Cayce created a cohesive understanding of the overall nature of the soul and the ultimate role of angels and spirit guides in the affairs of humankind. Each individual is here for a reason; that reason is to somehow bring spirit into the earth. Ultimately, humans, spirit guides, and the angelic realms all share in that collective purpose. As souls having a physical experience, the goal of each individual is to somehow become aware of the higher spiritual self and enable that divine nature to express itself in the material world. In terms of angels and spirit guides, they exist as divine messengers, guides, and spiritual comforters who are best at coming to the aid of individuals when spirit decides they are necessary at any given time.

Life is a purposeful experience. The Cayce readings suggest that whatever is occurring in an individual's life is occurring for a reason. Sometimes that experience forces an individual to draw upon resources he or she did not know they possessed; on other occasions, individuals choose even the greatest challenge at a soul level with the understanding that at some point they may help others overcome the very same experience. The end result is that the purpose becomes one of spiritual growth and personal transformation. Regardless of what is occurring in a person's life, however, the divine stands ready to be of assistance. Cayce repeatedly confirmed that "He has given his angels charge concerning thee, lest at any time thou dash thy foot against a stone," suggesting that even when the challenges of life occur, God and His divine messengers stand at the ready, willing to be of assistance. Truly, however, individuals may never come to the realization that spirit has always been present.

In 1941, during a reading given by Edgar Cayce to attendees of the tenth annual membership meeting of his association, a series of questions were asked about souls becoming "entangled" in the solar system and in other realms besides the spirit realm. Cayce began by confirming that whenever souls lived in accord with their spiritual essence, they essentially became constructive co-creators with the divine; when they did not, they essentially became a destructive influence: "For, we are joint heirs with that universal force we call God—if we seek to do His biddings. If our purposes are not in keeping with that Creative Force, or God, then we may be a hindrance . . . " (5755-2)

The same reading went on to suggest that not every soul was entangled in the material world: some souls who had been previously entangled had achieved enlightenment ("masters to whom there has been attainment"); there were fallen angels who chose to become a "cooperative influence" with the spirit of rebellion; and there were angels and archangels who have never left an awareness of the divine in the first place. Ultimately, however, everything was a part of God: "Without Him there was not anything made that was made," and eventually everything must return to an awareness of divine consciousness. At the highest level, the role of angels and spirit guides is to ever assist in the attainment of that goal.

Both the Cayce readings and scripture attest to the relentlessness of the Creator in terms of seeking after and reaching out for His spiritual children until all have regained enlightenment and returned to an awareness of their oneness with God. In terms of biblical confirmation, in addition to the parable of the hundred sheep and the shepherd pursuing even one that is lost, though ninety-nine remain in the fold (Luke 15:3-7), we also have the parable of the leavened bread: "The kingdom of heaven is like unto leaven, which a woman took, and hid in three measures of meal, till the whole was leavened," (Matt. 13:33) as well as the parable of the lost piece of silver:

> Either what woman having ten pieces of silver, if she lose one piece, doth not light a candle, and sweep the house, and seek diligently till she find it?
> And when she hath found it, she calleth her friends and her neighbors together, saying, Rejoice with me; for I have found the piece which I had lost.
> Likewise, I say unto you, there is joy in the presence of the angels of God over one sinner that repenteth.
> Luke 15:8-10

In terms of personal spiritual growth and the uncertainty individuals sometime hold in mind in terms of attaining that goal, Edgar Cayce reminded the original study group that there was a spiritual resource ever standing ready: " . . . hence the injunction 'Be not dismayed;' remembering that He hath given His angels charge concerning thee, that thine guide, thine guard, is ever in His presence . . . " (262-31). During a reading given to a thirty-five-year old lawyer, Cayce also insinuated that the end result envisioned by the Creator was only a matter of time:

> . . . The reincarnation or the opportunities are continuous until the soul has of itself become an *entity* in its whole or has submerged itself . . . That's why the reincarnation, why it reincarnates; that it *may* have the opportunity. Can the will of man continue to defy its Maker? 826-8

Angels and the angelic forces are part of the divine spirit that serve as messengers and intermediaries. When a seventy-nine-year-old man asked Edgar Cayce: "Do I have any direct guidance from invisible helpers?" The response was to the point, " . . . ever the guardian angel stands before the throne of God—for each individual." (3189-3) The readings are adamant in their perspective that each soul is made in the image of God and possesses the unique ability to become conscious of its relationship to the Creator. On one occasion, a reading suggested that the body, mind, and spirit were the vehicles for attaining divine consciousness in the earth, whereas the spiritual counterparts that were ever-present in spirit to assure that attainment were: each soul's innate possession of the Christ Consciousness (the awareness of the soul's oneness with God), the divine spark or Holy Spirit that remained as a part of the soul, and that soul's guardian angel. (2246-1)

In terms of fallen angels, the premise in the Edgar Cayce material is very different than that perceived by most individuals. It is not that some dualistic forces exist that are constantly vying for the souls of humankind, rather there is an internal struggle within each individual between doing things in accord with spiritual laws and reaching out to be of service to others, or choosing selfishness instead and remaining concerned only with one's personal needs. Essentially, it is the struggle between the Lower and Higher Self. The readings suggest that there are those in the angelic realms who have taken the role of oversight and even shepherding in terms of those individuals who continue to choose a rebellious stance. Eventually, even those who have chosen the spirit of rebellion will be brought in alignment with the Oneness of God for ultimately, in all of Creation, there is only God. It is simply our own rebelliousness that creates pain and personal challenge, some of which become our personal hell on earth. As one reading put it, "From what may *anyone* be saved? Only from themselves! That is, their individual hell; they dig it with their own desires!" (262-40)

Repeatedly, the Cayce material also confirms the presence and availability of spirit guides that may come as helpers, guardians, and intermediaries. At the same time, however, the readings frequently cautioned individuals against trying to contact either spirit guides or angels directly. Individuals were encouraged to instead attune to the Christ Spirit or God Consciousness, and if the divine felt that a spirit guide or angel could be of assistance, the messenger would be sent.

We are all on a spiritual journey. Although each of our journeys is very different due to previous experiences, choices, and the fact that we have all had occasions in which we have lived in accord with divine laws as well as times in which we have attuned more to the spirit of rebellion, we are all headed toward the very same goal. Throughout history, angels and the angelic forces have attempted to guide the human creature on its pathway toward that end. For some, it is called enlightenment; some call it atonement; some call it paradise, and some call it heaven, but the Cayce readings affirm it is not so much a final destination as it is a process of personal development: " . . . For you grow to heaven, you don't go to heaven. It is within thine own conscience that ye grow there . . . " (3409-1)

May the spark of the divine presence ever guide you toward that journey home.

Bibliography

Church, W.H. *The Lives of Edgar Cayce.* Virginia Beach, VA: A.R.E. Press, 1995.

Doctrine and Covenants. Salt Lake City: Church of Jesus Christ of Latter Day Saints, 2013.

Hamilton, Edith and Huntington Cairns, eds. *Plato: The Collected Dialogues.* New York: Pantheon Books, 1961.

Irving, Washington. *Life of Mahomet.* New York: E.P Dutton and Company, Inc. 1915.

Isaac, Stephen. *Songs from the House of Pilgrimage.* Boston: Branden Press, 1971.

Kelly, Sean and Rosemary Rogers. *Saints Preserve Us!* New York: Random House, 1993.

New Catholic Encyclopedia. Washington, DC: Catholic University of America, 1967. Vol I: A to AZT, s.v. "Groupings of Angels."

Newhouse, Flower. *Here Are Your Answers (Volume III).* Escondido, CA: Christward Ministry, 1983.

Parente, Fr. Alesslio, O.F.M., Cap. *"Send Me Your Guardian Angel" Padre Pio.* Amsterdam, NY: The Noteworthy Co, 1983.

Puryear, Herbert B., PhD. *The Edgar Cayce Primer.* New York: Bantam Books, 1982.

Smith, A. Robert, compiler and editor. *The Lost Memoirs of Edgar Cayce.* Virginia Beach, VA: A.R.E. Press, 1997.

Swedenborg, Emanuel. *Heaven and Its Wonders and Hell.* New York: Swedenborg Foundation, 1964.

The Jewish Encyclopedia: A Descriptive Record of the History, Religion, Literature and Customs of the Jewish People from Earliest Times to the Present Day. London: Funk and Wagnalls Co., 1901.

Todeschi, Kevin J. *Edgar Cayce on Soul Symbolism.* Virginia Beach, VA: Yazdan Publishing, 2003.

———. *Edgar Cayce on the Akashic Records.* Virginia Beach, VA: A.R.E. Press, 1998.

A.R.E. PRESS

Edgar Cayce (1877–1945) founded the non-profit Association for Research and Enlightenment (A.R.E.) in 1931, to explore spirituality, holistic health, intuition, dream interpretation, psychic development, reincarnation, and ancient mysteries—all subjects that frequently came up in the more than 14,000 documented psychic readings given by Cayce.

Edgar Cayce's A.R.E. provides individuals from all walks of life and a variety of religious backgrounds with tools for personal transformation and healing at all levels—body, mind, and spirit.

A.R.E. Press has been publishing since 1931 as well, with the mission of furthering the work of A.R.E. by publishing books, DVDs, and CDs to support the organization's goal of helping people to change their lives for the better physically, mentally, and spiritually.

In 2009, A.R.E. Press launched its second imprint, 4th Dimension Press. While A.R.E. Press features topics directly related to the work of Edgar Cayce and often includes excerpts from the Cayce readings, 4th Dimension Press allows us to take our publishing efforts further with like-minded and expansive explorations into the mysteries and spirituality of our existence without direct reference to Cayce specific content.

A.R.E. Press/4th Dimension Press
215 67th Street
Virginia Beach, VA 23451

Learn more at EdgarCayce.org. Visit ARECatalog.com to browse and purchase additional titles.

ARE PRESS.COM

EDGAR CAYCE'S A.R.E.

Who Was Edgar Cayce?
Twentieth Century Psychic and Medical Clairvoyant

Edgar Cayce (pronounced Kay-Cee, 1877-1945) has been called the "sleeping prophet," the "father of holistic medicine," and the most-documented psychic of the 20th century. For more than 40 years of his adult life, Cayce gave psychic "readings" to thousands of seekers while in an unconscious state, diagnosing illnesses and revealing lives lived in the past and prophecies yet to come. But who, exactly, was Edgar Cayce?

Cayce was born on a farm in Hopkinsville, Kentucky, in 1877, and his psychic abilities began to appear as early as his childhood. He was able to see and talk to his late grandfather's spirit, and often played with "imaginary friends" whom he said were spirits on the other side. He also displayed an uncanny ability to memorize the pages of a book simply by sleeping on it. These gifts labeled the young Cayce as strange, but all Cayce really wanted was to help others, especially children.

Later in life, Cayce would find that he had the ability to put himself into a sleep-like state by lying down on a couch, closing his eyes, and folding his hands over his stomach. In this state of relaxation and meditation, he was able to place his mind in contact with all time and space—the universal consciousness, also known as the super-conscious mind. From there, he could respond to questions as broad as, "What are the secrets of the universe?" and "What is my purpose in life?" to as specific as, "What can I do to help my arthritis?" and "How were the pyramids of Egypt built?" His responses to these questions came to be called "readings," and their insights offer practical help and advice to individuals even today.

The majority of Edgar Cayce's readings deal with holistic health and the treatment of illness. Yet, although best known for this material, the sleeping Cayce did not seem to be limited to concerns about the physical body. In fact, in their entirety, the readings discuss an astonishing 10,000 different topics. This vast array of subject matter can be narrowed down into a smaller group of topics that, when compiled together, deal with the following five categories: (1) Health-Related Information; (2) Philosophy and Reincarnation; (3) Dreams and Dream Interpretation; (4) ESP and Psychic Phenomena; and (5) Spiritual Growth, Meditation, and Prayer.

Learn more at EdgarCayce.org.

What Is A.R.E.?

Edgar Cayce founded the non-profit Association for Research and Enlightenment (A.R.E.) in 1931, to explore spirituality, holistic health, intuition, dream interpretation, psychic development, reincarnation, and ancient mysteries—all subjects that frequently came up in the more than 14,000 documented psychic readings given by Cayce.

The Mission of the A.R.E. is to help people transform their lives for the better, through research, education, and application of core concepts found in the Edgar Cayce readings and kindred materials that seek to manifest the love of God and all people and promote the purposefulness of life, the oneness of God, the spiritual nature of humankind, and the connection of body, mind, and spirit.

With an international headquarters in Virginia Beach, Va., a regional headquarters in Houston, regional representatives throughout the U.S., Edgar Cayce Centers in more than thirty countries, and individual members in more than seventy countries, the A.R.E. community is a global network of individuals.

A.R.E. conferences, international tours, camps for children and adults, regional activities, and study groups allow like-minded people to gather for educational and fellowship opportunities worldwide.

A.R.E. offers membership benefits and services that include a quarterly body-mind-spirit member magazine, Venture Inward, a member newsletter covering the major topics of the readings, and access to the entire set of readings in an exclusive online database.

Learn more at EdgarCayce.org.

EDGARCAYCE.ORG